'The man who has experienced shipwreck shudders even at a calm sea.'

— Ovid

'The fishermen know that the sea is dangerous and the storm terrible, but they have never found these dangers sufficient reason for remaining ashore.'

— Vincent Van Gogh

THE LUCKIEST THIRTEEN

A True Story of a Battle for Survival in the North Atlantic

by

Brian W. Lavery

This new edition, 2023

Barbican Press, London, Los Angeles and Lowestoft

First published in Great Britain by Barbican Press in 2017

Copyright © Brian W. Lavery 2023

Registered office: 1 Ashenden Road, London E5 0DP

www.barbicanpress.com
@barbicanpress1

www.brianwlavery.com
@brianlavery59

Cover by Rawshock Design

A CIP catalogue for this book is available from the British Library

ISBN: 978-1-909954-86-1

BARB
ICAN
PRESS

by the same author
The Headscarf Revolutionaries – (Barbican Press, 2015)

I dedicate this book to the memory of my friend:

Mark Kenneth Clough (1960-2015)
– Husband, father, grandad, brother, son and journalist.

He was a lover of books – and the works of Mr Ian Dury.

My best pal and my best man.
I now have one reason fewer to be cheerful.

CONTENTS

x   Contents

FOREWORD

This book tells a story that wasn't told properly at the time – the incredible tale of the *St Finbarr*, a new stern trawler that had smashed the national catch record on her maiden voyage and which, on Christmas Day 1966, was fishing off the Grand Banks in the waters of Newfoundland.

There was no news on that day on either of the two TV channels and no newspapers printed during the three-day festive break.

The disaster that befell the *St Finbarr*, the amazing courage of her crew and of the trawlers that went to her assistance, eventually made the papers, but it was only briefly front-page news outside the fishing communities where death and heroism were constant companions.

Brian W Lavery's deep knowledge and understanding of the men of the Hessle Road community who fished – and the incredibly strong women who waited, worked and grieved – has already been displayed in *The Headscarf Revolutionaries* (Barbican Press, 2015).

That book at last did justice to the battle waged by those women for better safety conditions in the late 1960s.

Now he tells a different story, one as gripping as any I heard during my twenty years representing what is now the ex-fishing community of west Hull. It's told with eloquence and empathy, displaying again the filmic quality that makes Brian W Lavery's writing so special.

How well I remember 1966. It was the year that England won the World Cup, The Beatles released their seminal album *Revolver* and Labour won the General Election.

I'd already been at work for a year, stacking shelves in Tesco. Had I left school with no qualifications aged 15 in west Hull rather than west London, I would in all probability have gone to the fish docks seeking employment as a "deckie learner" on one of the hundreds of trawlers that chugged in and out of the Humber Estuary during the heyday of the fishing industry. For these trawlers, the North Sea was a highway.

Their nets weren't cast until they reached the Barents Sea, Bear Island, Spitsbergen, the North Cape, or Newfoundland; the most inhospitable seas on Earth – as far north as man could go before the ice prevented them going further.

While other distant water ports such as Grimsby, Fleetwood and Aberdeen also fished in near and middle waters, Hull trawlers only ever fished in Arctic conditions. If there was moisture in the air it would freeze on the trawler masts, triggering a frantic race by the men to climb high to chop the ice away before "top ice" overturned the vessel, tipping its crew into water so cold that their blood would freeze within a few minutes.

On Christmas Day 1966, supermarkets were closed. Like almost everybody else, I had at least one day free of work.

Not so the fishermen who carried on working until the hold was full. The men spent three weeks at sea and were home for three days before setting out again. For the new stern trawlers, voyages were longer still.

They received a share of the catch so the incentive was to be at sea as long as possible catching cod and halibut and haddock. If the three days ashore happened to coincide with Christmas Day or some other holiday, they took it off; if it didn't, they could be found thousands of miles from the Humber working beneath the Northern Lights.

Alan Johnson, ex-Hull West and Hessle MP and former Labour Cabinet minister. Author, *This Boy Please Mister Postman* and *The Long and Winding Road.*

AUTHOR'S NOTE

On Christmas Day 1966, a fireball explosion ripped through the super-modern Hull trawler *St Finbarr* in wild Arctic waters on Newfoundland's Grand Banks. Ten men from a crew of twenty-five died instantly. Two more perished in the subsequent desperate rescue bid.

A two-day battle to save the blazing vessel followed as she was towed by Hull trawler *Orsino* which also carried survivors from the blast. Back in Hull, twenty-five anguished families did not know if their loved ones were dead or alive. A news blackout was caused by atrocious weather that blighted radio communications.

The word "prequel" grates with me – but if creative nonfiction can have such a thing, then this is it. This story, which I pieced together over the past two years, arose during research for my previous book, *The Headscarf Revolutionaries*, which told of the Hull Triple Trawler Disaster of 1968 and the subsequent fishwives' uprising. Those events overshadowed the disaster at the heart of this story – and led to the forgotten men of *St Finbarr* becoming a footnote in our maritime history. I hope I have remedied that.

This book, which tells of this disaster fully and properly for the first time, is a detailed, dramatised synthesis of news cuttings, court archives, radio reports, interviews and eyewitness accounts. Most dialogue was derived from these sources. Although it is written in a creative prose style and uses dramatic techniques, *The Luckiest Thirteen* is as it happened.

I owe the men of *St Finbarr* the duty of truth and hope this story sees that duty fulfilled.

Brian W Lavery, Hull

ABOUT THE AUTHOR

Born in Glasgow's East End, **Brian W. Lavery** forged a successful career as a journalist before undertaking a first-class joint honours degree (English and Creative Writing) and a PhD in Creative Writing at the University of Hull. His account of Hull's triple trawler disaster, *The Headscarf Revolutionaries,* brought national attention to previously untold lives of heroism. It has been optioned for film and spawned BBC TV and radio documentaries, song cycles, and a poetry collection. In August 2020 Dr Lavery received the *City of Kingston upon Hull Lord Mayor's Civic Crown Award* for preserving his adopted city's heritage. He lectures in creative writing and journalism at the University of Leeds Lifelong Learning Centre, and is features writer for *Fishing News* and several other publications.

PROLOGUE

Before the late eighteenth century, if you didn't like your fish salted you could either catch it yourself or live very near the sea.

In those early days London was well placed. With suitable fishing grounds off Essex, Kent and the south coast, fish could be taken from net to Londoner's plate in a day or so. Even then trawling was the most efficient way of catching – and with it came the overfishing and subsequent seeking of new grounds which was – and remained – part and parcel of the industry. The smacksmen of the time, victims of their own success, sought new grounds and found themselves trawling the North Sea.

A typical smack would be crewed by a skipper (usually its owner) and a small crew drawn from family, friends or neighbours. Very soon fishing was to boom, and Hull would lead the way. In 1843 – in a fish trade parallel to the Californian Gold Rush – the Yorkshire port was to be mobbed with fishermen seeking their fortune.

It was said that one of the Brixham-crewed vessels trawled approximately sixty miles from the mouth of the

River Humber and got caught in terrible weather, which it managed to dodge before it was blown off course to a new unfamiliar ground. Then the "miraculous catch" was landed and the legend continued that the sides of the vessel that hauled it in were covered with the silver scales from the mass of fish.[1] Trawlermen even nicknamed one of the grounds within the new Silver Pits "California" because of the prosperity it brought.

The 1851 Census shows that there were more than 1,000 people from Cornwall and Devon settled in Hull. In the 1850s more fishermen from the South West made their way north as the trade in Hull boomed. Among them were Richard Hamling and Robert Hellyer, names to be long associated with the industry. That's what fishing had become – an industry. Before the proliferation of the steam trawler towards the end of the nineteenth century, "fleeting" was the main way fish was brought to land. Smacks hauled the fish in by hand. Boxed fish would be stacked dozens high on open boats that were rowed to a waiting steam cutter for swift transfer to port. Fleeting was done in all weathers and the death tolls were spectacular, most lives being lost during these dreadful, dangerous but necessary transfers. In May 1883, at least 255 men were lost (this is a low-end estimate; others had it as high as 360) and forty-three smacks sank with all hands. Hull was worst hit with the loss of twenty-six smacks and 129 men and boys, accounting for six per cent of the whole workforce. In December 1894, Hull lost 106 men in one day. One the reasons for the lack of complete statistical accuracy is that many of the boys (and men) were often drawn from the workhouse; effectively non-persons whose demise was often neither noted nor felt.[2] When steam became king, the industry became not only safer but more efficient, but it was still the most dangerous of jobs. The loss of men remained higher than in any other occupation, three times more dangerous even than coal mining, a blight that was to stay with it well into the twentieth century.

A fish supper was no longer the preserve of the well-off or those nearest the water. Fishing caught up with the Industrial Revolution. Railways could take catches inland across the country. Fish landed in Hull in the early hours could now provide the evening meal for the hungry factory worker in Leeds, the weaver girl in Manchester or the coal miner in south Yorkshire and beyond. Sometime in the 1870s fish and chips became the national dish. The high proportion of women and girls both sides of the Pennines working in the textile trade encouraged the boom of the fish 'n' chip shop, which provided ready-made affordable food for their families. By 1913, there were more than 25,000 fish 'n' chip shops across the UK responsible for putting away more than a quarter of the 800,000 tons of fish that was Britain's annual catch.[3] That year, Hellyer Bros of Hull carried out successful experiments with the new Marconi Marine Radio systems and within a few years all fleets were using radios. The Great War (1914-18) saw many trawlers requisitioned as minesweepers by the Admiralty. Almost 800 carried out war service from Hull and Grimsby. In 1915, only a quarter of the Hull fleet remained fishing, and most had transferred to the western port of Fleetwood. In the war, more than 200 British trawlers were lost, sixty-two of them in service of the Royal Navy.

Like the Brixham men before them who moved on to the Silver Pits, the end of the Great War brought moves further afield for the industry, and the distant Arctic/North Atlantic fisheries took preference over the North Sea grounds from 1919. Hellyers finally ceased "fleeting" with their boxing fleets as others had done. Fish landed was worth £2,500,000 that year Hull and its fleet was established as the biggest deep-sea fishery on Earth.

Trawlers were now dispatched to Iceland, the Norwegian and Danish coasts, and to a lesser extent the coasts of Labrador and Greenland. Between the world wars business boomed again. From 1922 to 1928, eighty-six large distant-water trawlers were built for owners in Hull. The lifeblood of labour for this vast industry came from the Hessle Road district of Hull, running parallel to the St Andrew's fish docks.

In 1939, the outset of the Second World War saw fishing stymied once more. The Admiralty again requisitioned trawlers as minesweepers and as anti-submarine patrol vessels. Out of the 277 vessels in Hull's fleet, 260 were taken by the Royal Navy, seventy of these were lost in naval service and a further eight lost in normal fishing work.

By 1946, new vessels were being built and the catch for that year was a massive 373,216 tons from a fleet of 136 ships.[4] By 1950, fish landed was worth £7,786,752 from a fleet of 160 trawlers. A year later the White Fish Authority was set up to develop and regulate the industry. It would no longer simply be a matter of pitching up at new grounds with a bigger fleet and a gung-ho attitude. In May 1952, the Icelandic government imposed a four-mile limit, cutting off

5,000 miles of prime fishing grounds. Iceland claimed the area was overfished and excluded their own vessels too. The UK hit back by banning Iceland from landing catches at British ports. The Cod Wars had stepped up.

Trawler bosses knew it would only be a matter of time before the Icelanders demanded further limits.[5] They were also aware of the surge of Soviet freezer factory ships that were scooping up millions of tons of many species with their giant, indiscriminate factory-fishing leviathans. It would take bold new initiatives to keep their lucrative, if precarious, industry afloat.

Owners were not renowned for innovating or embracing new technologies; in fact, they "squeezed and sweated" every asset they ever had, including thousands of men who sailed never to return. By the 1960s most vessels fishing from Hull were still sidewinder trawlers, many of them decades old – indeed the last of the old coal-burning ships were not laid up until as late as 1962, which was just one year after the new Icelandic twelve-mile limit was accepted by the UK. In 1960s Hull, a handful of combines controlled the industry, some still bearing the names of those old Brixham adventurers who had come to Hull seeking – and finding – fortunes.

Grimsby-based Ross Foods Group took over Hudson Brothers Trawlers, making a new combined fleet of twenty-two. In 1961, Hellyers merged with Associated Fisheries, whose Lord Line fleet was made up of twenty-one vessels, making a total group of sixty trawlers. T Hamling and Company (eleven trawlers) and Boyd Line Ltd (twelve trawlers) formed a joint management firm to run their combined businesses from one office. So now, just three groups controlled 105 of the 141 distant-water Hull trawler fleet. With the often-outdated and always over-exploited sidewinder distant-water fleet there were many downsides. Fish had to be iced over at sea and brought back in a matter of days to market. Sidewinders had a limited range and could only be at sea for about twenty days, dependent on engine power. The new stern freezer trawler could be at sea for months and given that her cargo was frozen there was no rush back to market. These ships could hold at least twice the amount of fish and were better able to withstand the atrocious North Atlantic and Arctic storms that had done for so many vessels in the past. In 1961 the first distant-water stern freezer trawler came to Hull. Built in Bremerhaven, The *Lord Nelson* was about thirty feet longer than a conventional trawler. It was also luxurious in comparison, with air-conditioned cabins, showers and bathrooms at a time when most fishermen still carried their own bedding aboard. However, only part of the *Lord Nelson*'s catch was frozen at sea.

In the offices of Thomas Hamling and Co, the board gathered to design and commission a new kind of stern freezer distant-water trawler. It would be able to go further for longer and be safer in the pursuit of better and bigger catches. These Hull men determined their new ship would ensure a future for the fleet, to fish Newfoundland's Grand Banks and beyond.

Hamling's rivals were at their drawing boards too.

The race for The Perfect Trawler had begun.

PART ONE

THE PERFECT TRAWLER

'It's no' fish ye're buying – it's men's lives.'
                                    – Sir Walter Scott, *The Antiquary*.

CHAPTER ONE

The young couple walked hand-in-hand along the dock-side road, oblivious to the gunmetal-blue Ford Zephyr that glided ever nearer. They were ten minutes into their date. The backdrop was hardly one for a romantic promenade, with the tall triple chimney stacks of smokehouses, drifting pungent smells from the cod liver oil plant, rows of terraced houses, the fish processing factories and background noises of the railway siding from where trains took thousands of kits of fish around the country.

The girl's heels scrunched little frozen pavement puddles underfoot. The boy steadied her on his arm. Behind them on the dockside of the River Humber the world's biggest deep-sea fishery went about its business. The couple headed to town and passed the most unlikely Lovers Lane, an alley-way that linked the dockside and the main Hessle Road, the heart of Hull's fishing community.

The light faded as it does on winter days. They were arm-in-arm under lamplight that flickered to life. Secrecy added to the allure of the lovers' tryst. The pair oblivious. From the distance, foghorns wailed warnings.

The middle-aged man driving the Zephyr was a picture of rage. The big car halted a few feet in front of the pair and the passenger-side front door flew open and narrowly missed the boy. The lad gripped his girl's hand tight and placed himself between her and the car. His instincts were to protect her.

'You! Gerrin 'ere, you Jill… Now!'

The boy's courage evaporated. The girl released his hand from hers and rushed toward the car. 'Dad, you're showing me up!' The powerfully built man grabbed his daughter's arm and pulled her on to the passenger seat.

'Gerrin this bloody car, you Jill! I'll bloody show you showing you up, girl!'

One look told the driver his daughter's fella was a fisher lad. The young deckhand had what locals called that "I've lost me 'oss" walk, the wide-legged gait that gave away the trawlerman ashore. And – in case there had been any doubt – the big quiff, tartan cowboy shirt, powder-blue suit with moon pockets and high-waisted, twenty-inch bell bottoms confirmed it. (Add a Stetson and he'd have looked like a dandy gambling cowboy caricature.) The lad tried his best to keep his nerve. His attempt at a steely stare was more rabbit in headlamp than Gary Cooper at *High Noon* as his Grace Kelly was dragged off by her big builder dad. Red-faced Jill was now crying as her father turned his ire on to the scared kid on the pavement.

'And you… What the bloody hell do you think you're doing? Who the bloody hell are you to be out with my girl? If I see you near my daughter again, I'll kick your arse from one end of Hessle Road to the other. D'you understand, ya little toe rag? She's only bloody fifteen!'

Jill's feeble protest that she was 'nearly sixteen' was met with a silencing glower.

The lad's even more feeble, 'Aye, Mr Taylor' was drowned out by the slamming of the car door as the big Zephyr sped off with Jill in it. Tony Harrison was left on the cold pavement to contemplate the abrupt end of a date that just moments earlier had promised so much.

It was "settling day" – when the fisher lads picked up their cash share of the catch from the trawler bosses' offices. Tony had met Jill outside the Smith & Nephew plant at the bottom of Hessle Road, where she had worked as a Nivea girl since leaving school a year earlier. He had been suited and booted, a wedge of money on the hip and a girl on his arm. He was looking forward to the first of his three days at home, after a twenty-one-day Arctic trip, with the kind of money a shore lad would have to work a month for. A minute earlier he was on top of the world. Now he was just a red-faced daft lad who wondered what had hit him.

'What the fuck are you looking at?'

Even two giggling teenage girls on the other side of the road were a match for him that day.

'Don't know, mister. The fucking label's fell off!' said the taller of the pair as they turned heel and ran off.

'Bollocks!' Tony mumbled, flicked back the Zippo's lid, lit his Park Drive Filter Tip and walked towards the Wassand Arms.

The short drive to Jill's home in St George's Avenue seemed never-ending as her dad repeatedly tore her off a strip. Each time she tried to answer, he seemed angrier.

'I ant done owt wrong, Dad.'

'Owt wrong, owt bloody wrong! D'you think I'm bloody daft? He's a bloody wrong 'un. A fisher lad? They're only after one thing.'

'He's not like that, Dad.'

'They're all bloody like that, soft lass.'

'Not Tony, though. He's just a lad I met, we ant done owt wrong.'

'I'm not daft, girl. I know him. He's that Harrison lad from Somerset Street. You just bloody stay away, you hear me? Just bloody stay away. Or I'll bloody make ya.'

Jill gave no answer. There was no point. Anyway, if he knew the truth, he'd have killed them both, she thought. Jill had been Tony's girl since she was thirteen. They met at the Teens' Afternoon Saturday Dance at the Hull Locarno Ballroom. Tony, then fifteen, was working on the production line at the Smith & Nephew plant, where they made Elastoplast, in the city's Hessle Road – the main arterial thoroughfare of the fishing community. He took the job after leaving school but his real wish was to go to sea. His oldest brother Keith was a radio operator and young Tony wanted the adventure of the ocean waves. The extent of Jill and Tony's romance then was a snog at the bus stop on the way home. They saw each other on and off until Tony went to sea as a "deckie learner" (trainee deckhand) – then, if they were lucky, they met once a month. That was the routine of a trawlerman – up to three weeks at sea, followed by three days at home.

It was hardly *West Side Story*, but in Jill's teenaged heart and mind it was. She was Maria to a real Tony. It was forbidden love. Unlike the cinematic fantasy, Jill and her Tony faced more than the wrath of the Sharks and the Jets with her tough, over-protective big builder dad.

As months passed, their romance was on and off. It may even have fizzled if Jill's dad had not stepped in so abruptly. In fact, they had just got back together again that day when he caught them. Her father was sure he had put paid to a burgeoning romance – but Jill was as stubborn as he was.

She was confined to her room to 'think about what she had done'. It was then that Jill hatched a scheme to be with her Tony forever.

She only hoped she would have the courage to go through with The Plan.[1]

CHAPTER TWO

'Steaming up the Humber with the tide
Spurn Point behind us, fish dock alongside
With two-thousand kits in hand, we're the only ship to land,
We'll be worth a bob or two on Settling Day.'

From the trawlerman's anthem, 'Settling Day' – Reproduced by
kind permission of songwriter Keith Gay (nephew of Ross Cleveland
commander Philip Gay).

November 8, 1964, Spurn Point, the Humber Estuary.

On the bridge of No. H308 *St Finbarr* was Skipper Tom
Sawyer. No uniform, gansey sweater, skipped cap or beard
for this captain. The 39-year-old skipper with the dark
widow's peak, famed for his dapper appearance, was in
suede slippers, open-necked shirt and moleskin trousers.

Sawyer was personally chosen for command of this
modern freezer ship by *the* greatest Hull Don[1] skipper of
all – Jack "Dasher" Ellis – the Hamlings ships' manager,
who was acknowledged as the best of the best before he

retired to take up the command of a big oak desk. To all intents and purposes Jack Ellis ran Hamlings and his bosses were very pleased he did. The owners thought that "Don" skipper Sawyer one of the best too. He was a Fleetwood incomer and son of one of that northwest port's most famous skippers.

Captain Harry Sawyer MBE received his medal for bravery while in command of a trawler-cum-minesweeper in the Second World War. (All trawler skippers were seconded to the Royal Naval Reserve.) Fleetwood men, like their Hull shipmates, had the sea in their blood. They often swapped ports in search of work. The traffic was more in the direction of the Yorkshire port – the world's biggest deep-sea fishery. Fleetwood, thirteen miles north of the great seaside resort Blackpool, had once been a considerable fishing port too. But by the 1960s, the Lancashire port, which mainly fished Iceland and Norway, was hit harder than many by ever-growing Icelandic fishing limits. Fleetwood's loss was very much Hull's gain when the Sawyer made their new home in Yorkshire. Although famed for its brave, skilled trawlermen, Fleetwood was in the shadow of the Humber fishery. It did have other industries (chemicals) that slowed its economic decline, as did, with sweet irony, the Lofthouse Confectionery Company, makers of the famous Fishermen's Friend lozenges. (In 1865, local pharmacist James Lofthouse developed a menthol and eucalyptus liquid for fishermen to take with them on stormy and freezing trips. At first the mixture was bottled, but the difficulties of taking glass bottles on to rough seas led Lofthouse to make it in lozenge form.)[2]

St Finbarr prowed nearer to her home port and Skipper Sawyer was not the only man aboard who didn't look like a working trawlerman. Below deck in the accommodation corridor all apart from those on watch were ready for home and looked ready for a night on the town, which they were. In cabins that made previous berths look like jail cells, men lounged, played cards and whiled the time away as they drew ever-nearer to Hull. They took advantage of shower facilities that simply didn't exist on some of the old sidewinders they had served on. Young lads smoked in the berths, dressed in the "shore uniform" of the fisher lad: cowboy shirts, cowboy boots and half-moon-pocketed, pastel-coloured jackets above bell bottoms – a look that made them stand out.

Country and western crackled through the speakers and the lads spoke of what they would do with the small fortune they would get on settling day. Older hands put bets on via the wireless operator to bookies in Hull, who knew they'd be good for the money. They all knew that a full hold of ready-gutted frozen fish would produce film-star money, with more than 450 tons in the hold, three times what a sidewinder could land, given that the old ships could only do twenty-one days and had no freezer facilities. By comparison, the men of *St Finbarr* were fishing in an ocean liner. She could be at sea for up to fifty days with no need to race home as the cargo could not go off, unlike on the sidewinder, where the fish was packed by hand with ice to keep it fresh. The lads looked forward to home for their "three-day millionaire" spending spree. The pubs, florists, jewellers, restaurants, cinemas, cabbies and tailors would do their best to relieve them of their windfall.

For the skipper, there was no salary, just a share of the catch. That said, there were no impoverished skippers. Trawlermen and their earnings – especially those of skippers – were the stuff of legend.

One story in Hessle Road lore involved the great Don skipper Jack "Dasher" Ellis who, while giving evidence to a Board of Trade inquiry, was asked by the judge how much he earned in a year. Upon his reply, the judge blurted, 'Why sir, that's three times what I get!' Ellis replied, 'It's a free industry, m'lud, and you're more than welcome to come and join me.'[3]

Earlier in the *St Finbarr*'s voyage, another fellow "who did not look the part" had been with the crew. This chap looked to be more at home at the wheel of a shooting brake than a trawler. Jonathan Watson Hall, the boss's son, was assigned to the maiden voyage to the Grand Banks to report back to the board on their biggest investment in a century.

Watson Hall senior, the Hamlings chairman, would not allow his son an easy ride. That was not the Hamlings way. And although the men would never admit it, they respected the boss for putting his son alongside where his money was. They grew used to Jonathan being aboard and soon he was as much one of the lads as an Oxbridge-educated boss's son could be. Jonathan, an economist, joined the family business after the Army. He had been a Lieutenant in the 3rd Carabiniers of The Royal Scots Dragoon Guards during his National Service. He later took a reservist commission as captain in the East Riding Yeomanry, the same regiment and rank as his late uncle Donald Hall, who had died a hero in the retreat from Dunkirk. Jonathan had been closely involved with the development of the *St Finbarr* from the drawing board to the boardroom where the finance was raised. The instructions were given to Clyde shipyard Ferguson Bros, of Port Glasgow, from where the stern trawler was launched in September 1964. The maiden voyage to Newfoundland was directly after sea trials in Scotland.

The mission was to seek out new fortunes under pressure from Russian Pushkin-class super-freezers that scooped up all from the seabed – and ever-increasing fishing limit demands from the Icelanders that would only further damage British fishing interest in years to come.

You did not need to be an economist like Jonathan to know that.

Six years before his *St Finbarr* adventure, the boss's lad's other notable exploits on water included being a part of the Oxford Boat Race team. Before that, Jonathan had been a silver medallist in the pairs in the Empire Games.

It may have been odd for the men to see Jonathan among them, but then Hamlings was not an ordinary firm. They literally and metaphorically threw Jonathan in at the deep end. He was not the first Watson Hall who had to sink or swim.

As a young man imbued by a sense of duty, he was aware of the giants on whose shoulders he sat, none more so than his heroic uncle. In 1933, Uncle Donald, then just twenty-one years old, was trusted not just with examining a ship's progress but was given a budget to have it built and put to sea. The result was the *Pentland Firth*, a sidewinder trawler that was to be a great asset to the Hamling fleet. She was the biggest and one of the most successful ships of her kind. Tragically, she would out-survive the heroic young man who brought her to be, who sea-trialled her and was skipper on her maiden voyage, assisted by an experienced mate. Less than a decade later Captain Donald Hall, East Riding Yeomanry (Royal Armoured Corps, Regimental Number 63007) was killed in action on May 30, 1940. He was just twenty-nine. Towards the end of May 1940, the East Riding Yeomanry was part of 145 Brigade. It consisted of the Second Battalion the Gloucester Regiment, the Second Battalion of the Oxford and Bucks Light Infantry, the First East Riding Yeomanry and some Royal Artillery. Their anti-tank guns were holding the town of Cassel as a rearguard for the withdrawal of the British and French army from Dunkirk. Donald was the second-in-command of C Squadron of the Yeomanry. By the twenty-eighth, Cassel was surpassed by the German army. But orders sent to the 145 Brigade to withdraw did not reach the British until the twenty-ninth, so it was not possible to withdraw until nine o'clock on that day. It was ten miles to the Dunkirk perimeter and the East Riding Yeomanry, as a "recce" regiment, was the last to leave at midnight. A route had been reconnoitred earlier to Watou but the retreat was very slow and it was daylight when the Yeomanry reached there. Whichever way they went they ran into German troops. They were overwhelmed and surrounded. Donald Hall was killed attempting to reach Houterque, north west of Watou.*

---

* The remnants of the regiment who got home numbered just seven officers and 200 other ranks. The rest were killed or were taken prisoner. Captain Hall, who fell at Watou, was buried in Hooton, Belgium.

Throughout the maiden voyage, Jonathan observed the new ship and its commander in equal measure and noted the success of both. Skipper Sawyer, like Uncle Donald, was a man who Jonathan admired. The young executive held the skipper in awe as he did Jack Ellis, his first mentor – the man responsible for much of the ship's design. During his time aboard he witnessed first-hand the commander's amazing fish-finding skill.

In often-atrocious weather Sawyer pushed the ship and crew into areas of the Labrador coast, which caused men to question and even curse him. But time after time the nets came back bursting-full. The crew did not know how to take Sawyer, not that he cared. In one breath, he could be kind, almost avuncular to young deckhands (he was even known to put on movie shows for the men) – but in a heartbeat, could flash into Bligh-like rage. During one massive haul, Sawyer was observing the men as they worked the winch dragging the catch when the slow, deliberate and careful hauling of the gear is vital. Jonathan was chatting, Sawyer was making small talk. From the wheelhouse Jonathan noted "a bit of frap" – it looked like the men were arguing. Loss of focus could be fatal. In seconds the skipper had gone. Jonathan was left at the wheel. Through the rain-lashed windows he saw a furious row played out in violent mime. He could not hear but did not need much imagination to realise the foul-mouthed tirade that cowed four hard cases back into concentration. For a moment, Jonathan thought the skipper was going to attack the men, such was his clear, visible rage.

Minutes later Sawyer returned with a cheery, 'All right, lad?' for Jonathan, before adding, 'they won't bloody well do that again!' With that, the massive 1,113-ton, 211ft-long, thirty-six-feet-wide trawler was back to working with the efficiency of a Singer sewing machine. *St Finbarr* was bigger by some thirty feet than most sidewinders, but some seventy feet shorter than the new emerging stern trawlers, which like the Russian Pushkin-class ships came in at about 300ft or more.

Ellis had put considerable thought into the *St Finbarr*'s design. He wanted the ship big enough to handle the massive seas but not too big as to draw unnecessarily on fuel resources. She may not be able to hold as much as a Pushkin-class trawler, but she could haul more often across the year. Ellis put crew accommodation amidships and the machinery stern far enough apart to give what he called a "dumb-bell" effect where the ship was balanced aft and hull, making it handle better in high seas. He used his hard-earned knowledge of the fishing grounds, of the ships he had commanded and the marine engineering expertise he had gathered to put the best ship he could on the water, and Jonathan saw her fulfil Ellis's promise during his time aboard. Ellis knew that the ability to climb and descend the waves was one of the most important aspects of a ship. He had a "Goldilocks" theory as to the size of the ship. The sidewinder was too small and ill-suited to the waves that the North Atlantic could throw up. The Pushkin-class Russian ships and the UK stern trawlers were too long. The old sidewinders were too short. Ellis felt the *St Finbarr*'s length was just right.

The handling of it at sea trials and during the maiden voyage proved conclusively that he was right on the money. Sawyer said it was the best-handling ship he had ever skippered. Ellis had also negotiated the fuel-efficient engine system, made by a division of Hawker Siddeley, the famous aircraft multinational. The Mirrless National KLSSM8 was fitted with a turbocharger that could produce 1,592 horse-power at 330 revs a minute.

Again, the engine was much bigger and more efficient than the old sidewinders, but smaller than the 2,400-horsepower fuel-burners used by the rival stern trawlers across the globe. This engine was capable of far greater fuel economy than anything else on the scene, while still providing the power required for long-haul trips. 'Power with Economy" was the manufacturer's slogan. The ship's four-blade propeller was controlled by hydraulics via the bridge, and a Laurence Scott generator was coupled to the engine's main shafting system with an output of 320 kilowatts at 220 volts of direct current. This also powered a 4.5-horsepower air-conditioning sys-tem, which had a control switch at the upper deck entrance. This air-conditioning gave the companionways a constant chill wind and kept the temperature low where the fish were gutted, frozen and stacked.

Only the manufacturer was as proud as *St Finbarr* chief engineer Hughie Williams was of that engine – more so, perhaps – as Hawker Siddeley spent tens of thousands of pounds on a worldwide newspaper and trade press advertis-ing campaign, complete with a large portrait photograph of the *St Finbarr* gracing magazines and newspapers across the globe. The text boasted: 'What does the name Hawker Sid-deley mean to you… apart from aviation? Hawker Siddeley engineering goes to sea too. This example of a stern trawler *the St Finbarr* owned by T Hamling and Co, Hull, is powered by a Mirrless 1,592 bhp…' It ended with the grandiose claim to be 'harnessing British creative engineering to the world's needs…'

With an initial cost of £425,000 – and finally near to £550,000 – Hamlings made its biggest investment and the super-trawler project was a family affair from drawing board to launch runway. The *Hull Daily Mail*'s shipping correspondent Robert S Wellings noted at the time: 'The name of a little-known Irish saint who died more than 1,300 years ago will soon be coming easily to the lips of Hull trawlermen. They will use it when they talk about the big, 230 feet all-freeze stern trawler which will glide into the Clyde at the yard of Ferguson Brothers (Port Glasgow) Ltd, tomorrow. The trawler is for the saintly named fleet of Thomas Hamling and Co, Ltd, Hull and at the launching ceremony Miss Alanah Watson Hall, daughter of the company's chairman and managing director, will name it *St Finbarr*. Appropriately – but by coincidence – the launch is taking place on the day after *St Finbarr*'s commemoration day.'[5]

One of the best aspects of her design was how much "easier" it was gutting the fish, compared to what the sidemen suffered. *St Finbarr*'s nets emptied on to a ramp that delivered the fish to waist-high gutting tables in the below-deck factory room where men stood to gut and process.

On a sidewinder, this was done on an open deck with men bent double in freezing, relentless weather for hours on end. On an earlier "work experience" trip Jonathan had noted how back-breaking the work of gutting fish was. Each man lifted the fish from the deck one by one, feeling its weight every time. Jonathan determined to ease that task if he could.

The *St Finbarr* system was later to be adopted by many more ships. The ship also had a vacuum piping system that fired the detritus from the fish (guts etc.,) out to sea. The only fault Jonathan noted was the failure of the system when extreme cold caused frozen blockages that had to be repaired several times at sea throughout that voyage. It would be back to the drawing board for this – but for everything else, the trip was a great success. Young Mr Watson Hall was transferred to the Lord Line trawler *Lord Nelson* as a passenger bound for Hull from St John's, Newfoundland. He came home early from the maiden voyage to make his report ahead of the new ship's landing.

The men of *St Finbarr* had it easier than all the sidewinder men who had gone before. Bedding was provided in modern air-conditioned rooms panelled in the latest Formica. (The air-conditioning came as a by-product of the massively power-ful cooling system that kept fish fresh in the freezer rooms. For all the luxury, it was the fish that came first.)

She was the trawler that the others would have to catch up. It was no accident that other owners put orders in for stern trawlers within months of her launch. There were no further orders for sidewinders from Hull after that.

As the *St Finbarr* prowed up the Humber, radio operator Dave Redshaw revelled in a room that was as much a tem-ple of modernity as the ship's state-of-the-art engine room. All the latest equipment provided by Rediffusion (also a TV company) surrounded him as he prepared one of the final transmissions to the owners. Amid the radio wizardry with space-age names were the REDIFON G341 mains transmit-ter, the REDIFON R408 mains receiver, the WOODSONS

NS 120S reserve transmitter, WOODSONS SPEY SP1 reserve receiver, AGA Type NAPM 5 direction finder and the two Rescufone emergency sets. Dave prepared to send his final message of the maiden voyage. It confirmed 488 tons and seventeen hundredweight for her 4,500-mile round trip – a new national catch record.[6] In a few hours Britain's most expensive trawler was ready to come in on the tide to land a catch that would be the talk of the dock. Uncle Donald would have been proud.

CHAPTER THREE

Monday evening, November 14, 1966.

Jill Harrison was feeling quite good about herself. Why wouldn't she? She had married the fisher lad she loved, her little baby Jane was all she dreamt she'd be and they were all together in their little two-up, two-down. That night, she and her Tony were due out on the town. He would be sailing soon, providing there were no more problems with the vessel. Tony's latest ship was the latest modern stern freezer trawler. It had already been delayed three times. Quite a few electrical problems had been reported. The ship's insurers don't let her sail until she is certified as safe.

Hopefully, this time it would be safe away, thought Jill.

Jill's mam and dad were watching the bairn so she and Tony had each other all to themselves. She was in her best going-out gear and doing her make-up in front of the little dressing table mirror.

'*Mrs* Tony Harrison, Mrs *Tony* Harrison… Mrs… Tony… Harrison…'

No matter how she said it to herself, or how many times, it still took getting used to – and Jill loved getting used to it. The Plan she had hatched almost two years earlier worked like a charm, almost. It had taken a bit of working out, but work it did. Dad had now actually grown to *like* his son-in-law. He had even bought him his carry-out crate to take to sea when the lad had been skint. Jill smiled at the thought. Not so long ago her dad would have killed Tony – or anyone else for that matter – who had dared to look at his little girl.

Now here she was, eighteen, married with a kid… MRS TONY HARRISON!

All grown up.

She thought back to the day her dad dragged her into the Ford Zephyr and left poor old Tony looking like a daft lad. After that, she had been confined to her room for weeks and was forced to promise not to see Tony. The promise was broken next time Tony was home from sea, and many times subsequently. Jill would get ready in her best friend's house, the one to which Tony sent his love letters, presents and telegrams. The secrecy and subterfuge was a drag. Jill's dad was a tough, stubborn man, but she knew what made him tick, what buttons to press. Her mam often told her, 'You two are too alike, that's why you're always at each other's throats!'

That's when The Plan formed in Jill's head.

At her dressing table, Jill thought of how she had schemed and carried out her grand deception. The Plan was daring, simple and effective and no-one could blame her for feeling quite chuffed about the whole thing.

As 1964 gave way to 1965, Jill was still secretly seeing her Tony each time he landed. Like all trawlermen, Tony was only back for three days every three weeks. Their secret trysts were too few, Jill thought. She looked forward to meeting her fisher lad on "settling days" – and she still got dressed up at her friend's house beforehand, the one who took delivery of all the pressies and cards, especially the telegrams telling when her boy would be ashore.

It was Jill's younger brother Rob who forced her hand. In a rare slip-up, Jill had left one of Tony's telegrams on her dressing table. It fell into "enemy hands" – when kid brother Rob swiped it. And – as is the habit of thirteen-year-old brothers – jeering and mocking was followed by blackmail demands.

'Ooh, look, our Jill's got a fella. I bet our dad would love to know…'

'Don't you dare, ya little…'

'Ah, ah, language, sis…' After much *"kissy, kissy"* mockery and thinly veiled threats, Jill made a deal and got the telegram back with assurances of Rob's silence. The best two-bob she'd spent. But she knew he'd be back for more. Kid brothers – and blackmailers – are relentless.

She could not go on like this. There was no way her dad would let her be with Tony, unless she put The Plan into action soon – and to hell with the consequences. She would just have to put up with her dad's rage. This would get her Tony and put paid to her annoying little brother in one bold move. She had to just gather her courage and go for it – like ripping off one of the Elastoplasts that were made where Tony had once worked. It took longer than she thought to pluck up the courage. In mid-April 1964 while Tony was fishing off the coast of northern Iceland, Jill decided to pick the right moment to ambush her dad and put her scheme into action. When that moment came, Dad was in the living room; Mam was "siding" the dishes in the kitchen. There was only Jill and him in the room.

Jill just went for it.

'Dad, I'm pregnant.'

The *Hull Daily Mail*, behind which Dad was hidden for most of the time, was thrown to the ground.

'You're what?!'

'You heard.'

Jill thought he'd have shouted louder, maybe even hit out at her – or indeed *actually* hit her. His initial stony silence was worse. He looked odd. A strange mix of hurt, anger, sorrow and disappointment. It seemed an age before he demanded to know who the father was. It was, in reality, just seconds.

'It's Tony, who'd you think?'

'I told you nowt good would come of seeing that bloody toe rag.'

The explosion that Jill had prepared months for did not come as she thought. She did not hear it all anyway. It was like she was in a dream or a movie, watching herself. Dazed by her actions, she seemed to be hearing only key words as angry phrases segued one to the other into a furious tirade.

'Little... bastard... neighbours... warned... kill him... where is the ... when I get him... he'd better do the right thing... should've belted him when I... what you gonna live on... what about yer mam... he'd better bloody do the right thing... '

For a second Jill was overwhelmed by her father's anger and disappointment.

'Maybe I should tell him I'm lying,' she thought. She reconsidered just as quickly. 'I daren't' – not if The Plan was to work.

MISSION ACCOMPLISHED!

Jill's dressing-table reverie was broken as Tony shouted upstairs, 'Hey, you Jill, you still not ready? All the pubs on Road will be shut by time you're ready, girl!'

She smiled again and thought back to the "settling day rendezvous" when she first told her boyfriend what she had said to her dad while Tony was at sea. The dumbstruck fisher lad was not a big fan of The Plan at first.

On that day – almost nineteen months earlier – a stunned Tony said, 'But Jill, you're *not* expecting. Why the hell did you tell your dad you were? He'll bloody kill me... and for nowt!'

'Well, we had better get pregnant pretty soon then, hadn't we? Being in the family way was the only way my dad was gonna let me be with you, Tony. You know what he's like. Any road, it's worked. Dad's already booked the register office for May 25. So, we better get started on that bairn!' Back at her dressing table, Jill shuddered and thought back to when she "officially introduced" Tony to the family. He had appeared at the door in his best suit. The quiff was oiled down a bit. His beery breath carried easily and wafted across the width of the Welcome mat.

'Have you been in pub? Today of all days, could you not just stay away from it? You smell like a bloody brewery.'

The sheepish lad looked plaintively with watery eyes.

'I wasn't going to face your dad sober. He's a right scary bugger!'

Jill glowered.

'You best come in, daft lad, and get straight to the bathroom and brush yer bloody teeth or summat.'

Tony rushed past a stunned and flustered Jill to the bathroom. Seconds later, from behind the door, came a plaintive plea. It was stage-whispered.

'Jill, can ya fetch me a paper bag or summat? I don't want to make a mess,' Tony said.

Jill dashed to the scullery past the waiting Mam, Dad and brothers and grabbed a plastic bag. The noises-off from the lavvy told them all that the Boyes store carrier bag in her hand was now redundant.

Jill hissed at them, 'Don't none of you lot dare say owt.'

She then dashed back to make sure she was there for her Tony. (And to ensure he wouldn't leg it.)

After what seemed an age, Tony nervously emerged.

Richard Taylor's prospective son-in-law, the deflowerer of his little girl, had proved every inch the daft lad he thought him.

'I should've run the bugger o'er that day,' he thought as he held out his powerful hand. He wanted to punch him in the face but had to make do with the crushing force of a handshake.

'Welcome to the family, my arse,' the lad thought as he took his place at the dining table in the front room, where Jill's mam sat with an expression that clearly showed the doubt she felt as to whether this guy was worth the best china – and the tureen from Hammonds that she kept for best.

Jill's latest reverie was broken once more by the clap of her powder puff case as it clipped shut in her hand. Mrs Tony

Harrison, proud mother-of-one, took a final glance in the dressing table mirror and went downstairs to join her Tony for their big night out.

In spite of it all, The Plan had worked.

Everything was fine, except that Tony would not be home for Christmas. The three delays, the three separate telegrams that had intermittently come to their little house in Flinton Grove (reading: 'DON'T SAIL ON THE A.M. TIDE. REPORT FOR NEW ORDERS') had put paid to their first Christmas and New Year together for the new Harrison family.

His ship was to sail in the early hours of Wednesday and was not due back until early January. Jill put that to the back of her mind. This night they were together and going out on the town.

Drinkers in Hessle Road moved in migration patterns like wildebeest on the Serengeti. As one herd drifted from pub to street to pub again, another replaced it and the process repeated, all day, every day on the main drag – and in the rabbit-warrens of terraced streets branching from it. The main watering hole was the Star and Garter (aka Rayner's), the pub with the longest bar in Hull – and it needed it. Everybody that drank "on Road" found their way to Rayner's at some point, it was the Alpha and Omega of all pub crawls. (Only strangers and the brewery called it by its proper name. It was named after its first landlord Henry Rayner, which did not trouble the latest landlord Charlie Knott, who was very happily kept busier than most in his trade.) Rayner's took up the full corner between West Dock Avenue and Hessle Road. It had entrances and bars on both sides. Its massive windows served to warn many an errant fisherman that his missus was on the way to tear him a strip for another ruined dinner. From the West Dock Avenue side, recently "settled-up" fishermen could be seen on their way to spend their percentage share of the latest catch, or even to drown their sorrows if "landed in debt".

Either way – and every day – the folk drinking in Rayner's could see their world go by. Not for nothing was the pub known as the "trawlerman's other office". The "three-day millionaires" – as settled-up fishermen were nicknamed – would be spending like men with no arms. They would be out and about day and night, usually with the taxi driver they had hired for the purpose.

Drivers would often match them drink for drink, in pub after pub, party after party, ready to move their fare to the next venue, unencumbered by any breathalyser laws. Cabbies were handsomely paid – tipped often and by many – throughout the mega hire. Many fishermen had "regulars" – cabbies who served them for years. Often the valued customers saw these drivers more than they did their own families. Many was the fishwife who made an extra breakfast, dinner or tea for the surprise guest passed out on the sofa or floor, who had ferried her husband and his pals from pub to party and back.

There was never any shortage of guys to join a paid-up fisher lad on the piss. Rarely was anyone in a bar more generous than a settled-up trawlerman. One of the big rituals was what was known as giving an "ovall" – the name given to a cash loan handed to an out-of-work shipmate, who would return the favour when needed. Rayner's was the key meeting place for this unofficial "fishermen's mutual aid". Some of the married lads hardly saw home. For the single lads this was more so. That was the way of the trawlerman, "three tides and away" – 36 days at home a year, in a good year. Packing in a month's leisure in seventy-two hours became the norm. There was no shortage of folk to take their cash. Rayner's was also a place of bribes, where out-of-ship fishermen surreptitiously gave cash bungs to certain ship runners (the men who provided the trawler crews), and where trimmers (the men who packed the fish at the quayside for market) were not short of drinks from skippers, keen to know their catches would get the "right treatment" and look best at fish auctions.

This bar was also a place of danger, in common with other pubs "on Road". In a heartbeat, the crowded bar or lounge could go from a swinging party to a Wild West saloon-style fight. It did not take much to start a brawl, especially if there were Grimsby men in – or worse still – skrobs. (Skrob was the unflattering nickname given to Icelanders, or indeed any foreign Nordic fisherman.) One minute they would be all "brothers of the sea" and the next they'd be at it like the Hatfields and the McCoys.

Local bobbies, who were also "privileged" customers, rarely arrested a fighting trawlerman. If they put away every fisher lad in a pub punch-up, it would soon put the guv'nor out of business – and then where would the local plod get a well-earned after-hours pint?

From the Vauxhall Tavern near town to the Dairycoates Arms a few miles up the road, there were dozens of pubs in between, including the Alexandra Hotel (the Alex), the Criterion Arms (the Cri), the Wassand Arms, the Inkerman Tavern, the Strickland Arms and the Lion – to name a few. A full-on pub crawl on Road was nigh-on impossible but the Hull fishing community, undaunted in its pursuit of a good piss-up, kept giving it a good go.

A young guy in his best "going out gear" would stand out a mile in any of these bars when they were full of older folk. Furnishings were bleak. Most men had grey suits or grey belted macs, older ones with grey trilbies, fedoras or flat caps. Even their complexions seemed grey. Permanent bluish-grey fag fug, with pipe and cigar smoke, put an almost sepia tint on most bars. The perma-cloud was a boon that covered the smell of sweat, fish and cod oil from bobbers, filleters and the pattie slappers (the unkind nickname for the lasses from the fish processing plants). Looking through a misted-up pub window on a dark night was like viewing moving frames of a monochrome film. When the fisher lads came in with their pastel-coloured suits, bright shirts and ties, it was like actors from a neighbouring Technicolor movie had stepped on to a black-and-white movie set. Multi-coloured fisher lads were accompanied by girls in garish knock-off versions of the latest Quant or Biba. Some of the girls' perfumes and hair-sprays battled for supremacy with the smoky fug that hung over them. When they had enough of boozing on Road, they could make their way to the dozens of social clubs dotted throughout the area and beyond. In these clubs, they could take in a "turn" and even have a meal, which, if it was "right posh" was usually served in a basket.

For those who wanted to drink beyond licensing hours there were not only the "stop-backs" that coppers turned a blind eye to (and often took part in), but also the "coffee clubs" which were neither clubs nor vendors of coffee, but barely disguised fronts for shebeens; knocking shops where pissed-up sailors, fisher lads and other denizens of the Hull night would be drawn in by the promise of a good time and the warmth of willing "doxy."[1] The landed fishermen – and those due to sail – accounted for most of the "migrating herds" on Road.

There were other players in the perpetual-motion per-formance of Road boozing. Bobbers, who worked to land the catches from the early hours at the fish dock, were regu-lar mid-morning drinkers. The pattie slappers, with varying shifts, would be lunchtime and teatime drop-ins, as would be the shop workers from the dozens of retailers of Hessle Road, which from start to end was just over four miles long. The girls from the factories and trawler offices added to the clientele. After-hours coppers drinking with the landlords completed the portrayal of the vast thirst of Hull's fishing community.

Compared to the pubs and clubs on Road, the Maybury was a touch of Vegas. For a start, it had floors that your shoes did not stick to, as well as live music, food in a basket and wine that came in bottles, which many took home and used as the base for a new table lamp. The Maybury was in east Hull, near some of the new Hull council estates, where a growing number of Hessle Roaders had moved follow-ing overdue slum clearances of terraces condemned since before the second war. Tony and Jill's pals had saved them a good table in front of the posh stained-glass window and not too far – or too near – to that night's acts.

Tony spotted his *St Finbarr* shipmates, Kenny Pullen and David Young, sitting with their girlfriends and others.

'O'er 'ere, Tony!' said Kenny, pointing to the lager and the Babycham. 'I've got them in, get yersen o'er.'

The lads and lasses squeezed up along the bench seat under the window to let Jill join them. Tony took a stool next to Kenny and across from David and the others. The table was about three feet square and looked smaller with all the bottles, glasses and ashtrays crammed on to it. There were the usual "comedy stylings" of the compere, a novelty act, another comic, the house singer and the star turn. All of them competed against the heckling, bingo announcements, meat raffle draw, din of the mob, and the clatter of trays from waitresses as they delivered dozens of scampi platters and chicken-in-a-baskets. Those looking for a posh lamp base ordered their Mateus Rosé. There were also the occasional cheers, not for the struggling put-upon acts but for the crash of glasses hitting a parquet floor; a poor flustered waitress flushed as red as the footlights on the stage next to her while she tried to clear the debris, amid shouts of "sack the juggler."

'Everybody's a fucking comic,' the waitress mumbled under her breath in what was not the best of stage whispers. A hush did follow – well, less of a din, at least – for the star turn, Eric Lee, frontman of Eric and the Aces, whose Roy Orbison numbers were a favourite with the young fisher lads from the same streets into which the young wannabe pop singer was born. Tony and Jill were big fans, especially since Eric only lived a few doors down from them in Flinton Grove.

A flash went off as Eric started with *Only the Lonely*. By the time he had got to *In Dreams*, the kid with the posh Leica was firing on all cylinders. Eric's eyes were protected and hidden by his Big O-style sunglasses.

The lad with the posh camera was a deckie that the lads at Tony and Jill's table knew from Road. (Smart German cameras were quite common among trawler lads, who did a month's spending a few days after every trip. Also, when they were skint they could pawn – or sell – them. The same went with new suits, Italian shoes, even motorbikes and cars. A Pontiac or a Plymouth was not a rare sight on Hessle Road.)

After the young cameraman finished with Eric's photos, he turned to the Harrisons' table. 'C'mon, say cheese everybody!' He grinned and caught the final image of the boys. The MC announced Eric would be back after the bingo and the meat raffle.

It was an unforgettable night at the Maybury.

The day after, things were back to normal for Tony and Jill. The bairn was back from her grandparents. Tony was due to sail in the early hours. For now, they were all together in their little two-up, two-down. Jill thought she'd wait until after she had given Tony his tea before she'd tell him her latest news. After she had sided the dishes in the small scullery she brought Tony another cuppa, handing it to him in his armchair near the fireplace.

'Tony love, I've got summat to tell you,' said Jill as she handed the cup to him. Tony took a sip.

'What is it?'

'I'm late, I think.'

'Late for what?'

'You know, late… ladies' things, you know.'

She watched as the realisation dawned on her young husband's face.

'Oh…'

'Is that it? Oh? Tony, you're gonna be a dad again. Well I think so, any road.'

'When?'

'I thought you'd be a bit more excited.'

'Of course I am, love. I'm over the moon, honest. It's just a bit sudden, like,' Tony laughed.

'What's so funny, you Tony?'

'At least this time we can tell your dad the truth – and he won't want to kill me this time around!'

He put down the teacup and pulled his young wife towards him on to the chair's arm.

'It's grand, love, just grand,' Tony said.

'Let's make sure I am expecting first for sure though, love, eh? I am going to doctors this week. I'll send you a telegram, letting you know what he says. Here's what I'll do. If it's a false alarm, I'll sign it "Jill" as usual. If not, I'll sign it "Jillian" – and then you'll know for sure that I'm expecting.'

'It's all a bit Secret Squirrel, Jill, eh?'

'I just don't want them on your ship knowing all our business. You know what they're like. Just look out for the telegram. Humour me.'

'All right, Jill, or should I say Jillian?'

00.30am, Wednesday, November 16, 1966. No. 2, Flinton Grove, Hessle Road, Hull.

Jill watched Tony silhouetted against the curtains as he lifted his kit bag.

'That's me off, love. You take care, darling, especially if...'

'I know, I will,' said Jill. 'Watch out for the telegram – and then you'll know if you're going to be a daddy again.' A car engine rumbled and rattled outside. Tony came to the bedside, leant over and gently kissed his wife for the final time. The bedroom door closed. Then Jill did something she had never done before. She got out of bed, went to the window and watched her Tony walk to the waiting car. That was a real taboo in the fishing community in which superstition was rife. Waving your man off was "waving him away" in the words of the old fishwives' tales. Folk outside the community may have found it easy to laugh as such nonsense, but those who lived in constant danger respected its superstitions if nothing else.

At that moment, the heartbroken young wife didn't care about daft superstitions. She pulled the curtains back slightly and saw Tony. He looked back to Jill and waved – something he had never done before either. Jill shivered a little and went back to bed.

'I shouldn't have done that; I shouldn't have done that. I just should not have done that,' Jill whispered repeatedly as she got back into bed.

'Bloody superstitions. Don't be such a daft lass,' she told herself.

She was comforted by being safe and sound in bed, with her baby who burbled in the cot and her true love going to sea to keep them cosy, unlike that poor homeless Cathy lass who had been on the telly earlier that night.[2] A fitful sleep followed for Jill with baby Jane at her bedside as her Tony headed out on his second voyage on Hull's top trawler.[3]

CHAPTER FOUR

*'They were fishing with ocean liners, the owners were having a spree
Fishing with ocean liners, scooping up every fish in the sea'*

From Fishing with Ocean Liners, on the McGarry Nelson CD 'Flowers on the Water', reproduced by kind permission of Hull songwriter Brian Nelson.

St Andrew's Fish Dock, Hull, November 16, 1966. 1am.

No-one on the dock could miss the perfect trawler – even in the cold winter's darkness. Her wheelhouse was to the fore, unlike the surrounding familiar sidewinders where the wheelhouses were amidships. The sidewinders – between 450 tons to 800 tons and usually 130ft long – were dwarfed by the modern super-freezer ship. She was ready to return to the great grounds of Grand Banks and Flemish Cap in the hope of another gigantic catch, on what would be the thirteenth trip since her maiden voyage.

St Andrew's Fish Dock was busy day and night, especially when the tide was high and ships readied for voyage. From the *St Finbarr*'s bridge Skipper Tommy Sawyer observed its buzz. Taxi brakes squeaked and headlamps caught the sleety, cold rain in the "V" of beams. Diesel engines on the quay-side and on the trawlers thrummed at differing volumes. Deckhands, many still pissed straight from the pubs, carried kitbags and booze-filled clinking carry-outs up gangplanks helped by barrow boys there for that purpose, as well some cabbies – there for one last drink with their fare.

Old shipmates shouted greetings and farewells. Ship runners – the agents who made sure vessels were crewed properly – were frazzled rounding-up men who were not yet ready to board. These runners ensured men were taken through the store and put on to the correct ship. It was always hectic. The stores opened two hours before high water, day or night. Men bought all they needed for their trips to Arctic waters; boots, gloves, knives, oil frocks, sou'westers, mittens and, for the side-winder crews, bedding. Crews paid for it all themselves. Many had no cash on them due to yet another superstition. It was thought to be bad luck to take money on a trawler, lest the sea gods curse you with a bad trip for such hubris. This was great news for the kids who hung around outside pubs or at taxi doors, as drunk – and even some sober – fisher lads threw their remaining coins to the pavement for the kids to fight over in what was known as a "scramble." Those who did not chuck their money away simply handed to the cabbie yet another tip, or gave it to their own kids before leaving home.

The fact the deckhand had not a penny when he got to the company stores was not a problem. It was the per-fect capitalist model; all the owners provided was a ship, berth and board – and the chance of "film star wages."

The men paid for the rest; from gutting knives to safety suits. The firm always took what was owed later from the trawlerman's pay. Many came home owing more to the firm than was earned. (It's from where the phrase "landed in debt" comes.) When a man had what he needed from the company store, he was rushed up the gangplank. All trawlermen could tell from a distance which ship was theirs, especially if it was one in which they sailed often. Each had a unique silhouette; not by happenstance but by Admiralty instruction.

In war, ship recognition in the most difficult of seas was vital. It is thought the idea of a silhouette recognition for each trawler followed the Russian Outrage of 1904 when part of the Hull trawler fleet was sunk in atrocious weather by the Russian Navy, which mistook the fishing vessels for the Japanese Navy's fleet.[1] Trawlers in wartime also often served as minesweepers for which ready recognition had obvious advantages.

On sidewinders, some cabins were not much better than jail cells and many of the sidemen brought their own bed rolls. In the older ships, they took paillasses aboard that they stuffed with straw, a practice going back a century. Many also brought foodstuffs like bacon, sausage and tinned foods, for when supplies on a sidewinder ran out near the end of a three-week trip, as often they did, all that was left was fried fish or an awful stew called "shackles" which you helped yourself to from a hanging pot in the galley. The men of the *St Finbarr* were in the lap of luxury by comparison.

From his bridge Sawyer heard a cacophony of shouts, wailing foghorns, and men clambering gangplanks, and he saw the dimly lit mouths of dockside tunnels from which the "bobbers" came to land catches. They were heard before they were seen, as they marched through tunnels from West Dock Avenue and Subway Street to the quay. The collective clatter of their clogs provided an improvised rhythm section to this dockland rhapsody.

The Hamlings ship's runner was in the wheelhouse.

'Red tape time?' Sawyer smiled.

"Fraid so, skipper,' replied the runner and handed him the "red tin" – the secure metal box that contained the paperwork for the voyage, bosses' instructions, insurances, orders, crew lists and the like.

First Mate Walter Collier was with his boss. The thirty-seven-year-old was a veteran of the maiden voyage, and had been with Hamlings for twenty years. He was Sawyer's right-hand man; the skipper, who was not a man for red tape, left a lot of the admin to him. The skipper opened the tin, took out some papers and perused the most important document for him – the crew list. He needed to know if his men were up to his high standards. He passed the remainder of the documents back to Collier. Sawyer also had to know how many were back from last time. There is no skipper universally popular with the men, and fewer still who courted popularity. A trawlerman in the bar might often curse "that bastard in the cod office" – but the real sign of the good skipper was if the men came back to serve under him. For Sawyer, this was more often the case than not. The runner looked up and took out a Park Drive, passed it to Collier and lit one himself.

'Not for me, thanks. But feel free,' Sawyer said.

The runner took a pull on his cig as the skipper looked through the list. It read:

Officers: Captain, Sawyer, T., Mate, Collier, GW.,
Chief Engineer, Williams, H., Second engineers,
Hardwick, T., Grinlaw, G., Wireless Operator:
Gray, T., Bosun, Samms, E., Greasers, Smith HW.,
Scott, JG., Sparehands: Petrini, E., Tognola, P., Evans, A.,
Bull, V., Pullen, K., Matthews, J., O'Dell, J., Hamilton, J.,
Harrison, A., Coulman, R., Sigurdsson, J., Brigham, S.,
Smith, J. (fish room chargehand), Young, D. (deck learner),
Cook – Prince, H., Cook assistant, Whittaker, D.

The eagle-eyed skipper noted that although a crew of twenty-five were all there and up to the mark, there was a replacement from the previous trip.

'Where's Bri Williams this time? Sick?'

'No, skipper – bloody superstitious. Called in saying he wouldn't go because of the three delays. Bad things in threes and all that kind of shite, said it were a bloody omen or summat. You know what they're like. Don't worry, though, he was replaced within the hour.'

'Oh well, his loss. We've had nothing but big pay days so far.'[2]

The mate took back the list from Sawyer and put it in the tin with the insurance papers, owners' instructions, pay details and other documents. He would read them when they were steaming out and keep his boss updated on anything he thought he'd want to be bothered with. Tommy Sawyer was interested only in that which got him the biggest haul – everything else was secondary.

Down in the galley the second most important man on the ship, cook Harry Prince, was going through his lists. If an army marches on its stomach, a trawler crew sails on hers, especially when the relentless shifts of eighteen hours of trawling, hauling and gutting got started in the frozen Arctic waters. (It was reckoned a sparehand needed at least 6,000 calories a day.) You never saw a fat deckhand. Harry Prince looked at the list and started reading aloud while ticking a paper with the pencil that seconds earlier had been behind his ear. The list read:

GREEN GROCERIES

30 bags potatoes (1 cwt)

20 stones – onions

12 stones – green veg mixed

12 stones – swedes

12 stones – carrots

2 stones – beetroot

12lb – dehydrated cabbage

After he read each item out aloud, Harry ticked the page and said 'check.'

After one 'check' a voice replied, 'mate' –

'Very droll, ya daft Wessie prat. Gerrin here and help me check these off.'

Dave Whittaker, a West Yorkshireman, from Leeds, had reported to the galley for duty. Fortunately, he and his boss got on well, in spite of Harry's exasperation with Dave's banter.

They had to get on, being stuck in a tiny – and often dangerous – galley (especially in high winds when anything not chained or fixed down became a hazard).

'Aye, aye,' Whittaker mocked.

Harry rolled his eyes and carried on as Whittaker took a copy of the list and the pencil from him.

'800lb beef.'

'Check.'

'120lb mutton.'

'Check.'

'120lb pork.'

'Ch…'

'Cut it out, daft lad. Just tick them off. We don't need Arthur Askey aboard.'

'I thang you!'

Harry's glower put paid to Dave's Arthur Askey routine.

'20lb sausage, 30lb oxtail, 20lb kidney, 30lb chops, 20lb liver… fetch the other grocery lists, Dave.'

Harry carried on reading as Dave checked his duplicate list. Running out of food would be a disaster, especially with a Christmas at sea coming up.

'Eight pounds, mincemeat, two tins of ginger, two packets celery seeds, ten bottles Yorkshire Relish…'

'Saucy…'

Harry frowned, but carried on, 'thirty bottles HP brown, thirty HP tomato, …' and ticked off a further fifty items, finishing with … 'thirty-six boxes jellies…'[3]

Harry was a heavy-set fellow known to have a very sweet tooth and a big fondness for jelly. So, Dave couldn't help himself.

'Is them for you then, Harry?'

'Very funny, Mr Comedian. Just make yourself useful and put on a brew, you prat.'

Dave smiled, knowing he had hit a little nerve. He moved across the galley to fill the kettle. More than once Dave and his shipmates had visited Harry's cabin and found numerous empty packs of Hartley's Jellies scattered there!

In the wireless room the new man made himself familiar with the latest in modern Rediffusion radio apparatus. Tommy Gray checked out the other ships in dock. A glance through his porthole reminded him just how good this ship and her gear was. Some of the old sidewinders had some ropey old Marconi stuff dating back years and, worse still, some of the ships did not even have wireless operators. Amazingly, this was not illegal. Provided a skipper had a radio telephony certificate he could sail without a "sparks" (the nickname given to radio operators).

Gray was a top man from a top ship, and had been sparks on the previous year's Silver Cod Trophy-winning trawler *Somerset Maugham*. (That trophy was given to the skipper and crew with the biggest annual catch.) The bespectacled fifty-year-old, a married man with three grown-up kids, had been a top trawler radio man for fifteen years and a hugely respected one. Most wireless operators were held in a kind of awe by trawlermen. Fisher lads knew a good wireless operator was worth his weight in gold and was also a man with whom a deckhand would not want to fall out.

Tommy Gray was one of the best. He had qualified as a radio operator, aged just 17. In the Second World War, he was commissioned as a second lieutenant in the Royal Navy and served with distinction from the rescues at Dunkirk, the evacuation of Crete and the Arctic convoys. For a brief spell near the end of the second war, Gray was seconded to the air/sea rescue services of the United States Navy, at the Waldorf Hotel in New York City. He could have had a full naval pension by his forty-fifth birthday, but chose to seek more adventure fishing the Arctic and North Atlantic seas. He was a quiet hero, a safe pair of hands in a crisis and a man that others admired. The men of the *St Finbarr* knew of Gray by reputation before he arrived on board for his first trip on the super-trawler. He looked forward to the challenge of the ultra-modern equipment in his new wireless room.

The sparks was not only in charge of the sending of telegrams and setting up ship-to-shore calls with home but, more importantly, was the bringer of racing results. The men saw him as having a cushy number, mostly sitting in a warm room while they froze on deck. In their eyes, all radio men were "boffins" and therefore the butt of macho deckhands' gags – not too many, though, unless they wanted to wait until they were ashore to know if they had won anything from the 3.30 at Goodwood. That said, it would be a brave deckie who would try to mock Tommy Gray.

His other main official duty was most important as it directly affected everybody's pay packet. It was part of the wireless man's job to process (boil) the cod livers that went to make cod liver oil. The money from the sale was split between the crew. This was known as "oil money." So, not only was the sparks a man to depend on, he was always worth listening to and keeping on side. He was the man they would need to make a Mayday call heard should the worse fate befall.

He was also the man who blasted music from the American Forces Network through Tannoys on deck and into the fish room as men relentlessly hauled and then gutted massive catches.

Strains of Johnny Cash, Patsy Cline, Alma Cogan *et al* provided the soundtrack for this back-breaking work, by men who saw themselves as frontiersmen of the sea. The oceans were their prairies. These were the cowboys of the deep.

No sea shanties or squeezebox music there.

The crew had been listening to Tommy's predecessor – Dave Redshaw – a lot. Redshaw had sailed with the *St Finbarr* from the voyage after the maiden to the one before Tommy Gray was hired. Over his eleven trips, Redshaw complained of several electrical faults on board, mainly because it was he who had had to repair them. On earlier voyages Redshaw had been called to the below-deck crew accommodation a few times to deal with fires caused by shorts and melted cables. Water had got into the ceiling panelling on another occasion and caused lights to short out. On one voyage, he smelled smoke and traced the source of it back to the main deck headlight in chief engineer Hughie Williams' cabin.

The chief, who had also been with the *St Finbarr* on her maiden voyage, forwarded Redshaw's reports back to Hamlings. Williams had also taken a break from the ship and had returned just three voyages back. The men, chatting, smoking and drinking on the deck, speculated that the previous sparks' reports were what held up the ship three times before that night. The lads were also not surprised to see a new wireless man.

The bosses were not too happy at their flagship vessel being seen as anything less than perfect. Redshaw, who had been on loan from the Rediffusion company, was said to have refused to come full-time with the *St Finbarr* because of a possible loss of superannuation – but the lads thought he was "elbowed". Gray would have known about his predecessor's run-ins with the office. He also it made it clear to chief engineer Hughie Williams that he would not be an ad-hoc electrician.

'Get a qualified man in or do it yourself.' Reluctantly, Williams, a brilliant and able engineer, took on yet another unofficial duty as ship's electrician.[4] He had liked Redshaw and had also reported his concerns to the bosses. Hughie Williams liked Gray too; Tommy was a man who spoke his mind – as was Hughie. Williams also had a distinguished naval war record and there was mutual respect between them.

Both the chief engineer and the previous radio man felt that the skipper should have pushed the bosses for a ship board electrician. To be fair to the skipper, all the electrical issues were dealt with in Hull. After the three delays in dock, the ship was passed A1 before voyage and its electrics certified fit for purpose. Skipper Sawyer had a reputation with some as a swashbuckler. He was brave and a great fish-finder. He did not understand folk who did not think like him. If you wanted a pal, Sawyer was not your man.

If you wanted a bulging pay packet, he was.

Hughie Williams was uneasy. He never liked Christmas at sea – and not just because he missed his family. In his cabin, the chief reflected on years back when, as a young engineer, catastrophe struck him and twenty-three other souls on Christmas Day when their ship ran aground off the Norwegian coast and sank due to a skipper's incompetence.

In 1947, Williams had begun his career with Hamlings after his war service in the Royal Navy. That year on December 19 his ship the *St Amandus*, a 443-ton, coal-burning steam trawler with a crew of twenty-four, sailed from Hull heading for the fishing grounds of the White Sea. The ship had previously served as a minesweeper and was demobbed by the Admiralty and bought by Hamlings.

After three days at sea, the ship's two echo sounders packed up. Skipper Robert Weightman decided to take his ship to Harstad to get them repaired. He was off the coast of Svino and plotted to go the 330 miles to Skomover on the southernmost tip of the Lotofen archipelago, an area riddled with underwater hazards.

Somehow the skipper – whose navigation was later described as "haphazard" – managed to miss his destination by thirty miles and had to steam back. After four hours, land was spotted and Weightman decided to set a course up the West Fjord. The fjord is lined with lighthouses: Tennholmen, Maloy Skrholmen and Flatoy, which Weightman had spotted, but unusually he failed to verify the ship's exact position before dropping anchor. Due to the massive snowstorm that had fallen upon them, the skipper was almost "blind" in the blizzard. The ship was laid-to all Christmas Eve. When the anchor was weighed as the storm

subsided, Skipper Weightman noted a "two-flash" light signal from what he thought was the Tranoy lighthouse and set
his course accordingly to avoid potentially fatal rocks.

What Weightman – who had been in the wheelhouse for
thirty hours straight – thought was the Tranoy lighthouse
was in fact the Skraaven. Both were "two-flash" houses.
However, Tranoy was six seconds between each flash and
Skraaven fifteen. A cursory glance by the skipper at the
Admiralty List of Lights or the *Norway Pilot* books in the
wheelhouse would have averted the disaster.

An hour later his ship crashed on rocks, which ripped a
hole in her side. Freezing waters gushed through into the
fish room. Panicking men in the below-decks accommodation scattered and scrambled up ladders on to the upper
decks. Weightman was in the wheelhouse with the mate and
two deckhands, one of whom was at the wheel as the ship
listed massively to starboard. The only lifeboat they could
get on was on that side.

Men were sent back below to drag masses of bedding
on to the whaleback. Before they all boarded the lifeboat
and lowered it to the fjord waters, the mass of bedding and
mattresses was set alight as a giant makeshift distress bea-
con. Flames leapt high from the doomed ship. The "bea-
con" worked. Within thirty minutes of rowing their lifeboat
from the stricken vessel, the whole crew was picked up by a
nearby "snibby" (a small net-fishing boat) that had spotted
the blaze. The snibby towed the lifeboat and the freezing,
sopping wet men ashore.

Ironically, the rescued crew spent the night in one of the
lighthouses their errant skipper had missed at Skraaven.

They were later moved to the local Seamen's Mission and then billeted with local families. After three weeks, they were returned to Newcastle on a ship from Bergen. From Newcastle, they travelled to Hull by train, all of them still wearing the gear they were in when they abandoned ship.

A Board of Trade Wreck Inquiry, chaired by Judge John Naisby QC on September 15, 1948, banned the skipper from sailing for one year. In the summing-up, Judge Naisby added, 'In our opinion the skipper was gravely at fault in that when the two-flash light was reported to him whilst the vessel was at anchor in a position which he had taken no care to fix with any accuracy, he assumed that this two-flash light was Tranoy, even though a cursory study of the chart would have enabled him to ascertain that at that distance Tranoy was unlikely to be visible. Moreover, he neglected to take any steps throughout the whole of December 24, 1947, to fix his position accurately either by means of cross bearings or four point bearings, and failed to check his position by taking a cast with his deep-sea lead. In other words, he erroneously and rashly assumed that the two-flash light he saw was the light which he was indeed hoping to see, and this wishful thinking combined with an almost wilful blindness to the indications which were staring him in the face was the cause of the stranding and loss of the vessel.'[5]

So, Williams's suspicion of skippers, even great ones like Tom Sawyer, was not entirely surprising. The chief engineer was more aware than most of how complacency could kill. But – like the other men of *St Finbarr* – Hughie came back to the Hull super-ship. The only thing Williams loved more than his work was his family. In his cabin were photos of his wife Mary and their four kids, all of whom would visit that same cabin each time Hughie came home. The younger kids loved exploring the little Formica-lined room that Daddy called home when he was at sea. He had been on the *St Finbarr* during her sea trials in Scotland and subsequent maiden voyage to Newfoundland. Before every trip Williams went through the same routine. The dining room table would be where the kids would gather as he emptied all his spare cash on to the tablecloth. Even a level-headed engineer respected the fishermen's superstitions.

'I want you all to share it fair now, you hear me.'

'Yes, Dad,' the kids would chime in unison. Mum Mary would join Linda, fifteen, Jeanette, nine, and little baby Paula, three, at the table to make sure the kids were diverted by the pennies to try to take their minds off their father's imminent departure. Oldest sibling David, nineteen, was too grown-up for such things now. They all joined in the leaving ritual each time Williams went to sea. There would always be the "welcome back" visit to the ship when he got home. That year was sadder, especially for the younger kids, as Daddy would be away over Christmas. The unspoken family rule was that there was never any waving or saying good-bye. That would be bad luck. Like all trawlermen's kids, the Williams clan respected the "daft superstitions" that deep-down few chose to ignore and fewer still would disregard. While her Hughie was at sea, Mary took comfort from the poems he composed for her, which she kept in her secret place.[6]

Out on the *St Finbarr*'s whaleback, as Sawyer made final preparations for the voyage, the remainder of the crew gathered and smoked, drank and chatted. Jack and Harry Smith were old shipmates and had served together many times. Fifty-four-year-old Jack and his pal Harry, fifty-two, had been at sea since they were kids. Harry had done the classic "run away to sea" at just eleven years old in 1925 when he managed to blag his way to a cabin boy's job. Jack, Harry often joked, was a newcomer, having only been at sea since the grand old age of fourteen. Harry was pleased but a bit surprised to see his old pal. Jack was a well-known bosun with Hamlings and had served for years on many of their sidewinders.

'Hey up, Jack. What you doing here? Have you replaced Newfie Samms?' Harry was referring to the *St Finbarr*'s Canadian bosun Eric Samms, a pal of Hughie Williams, who had been with Hamlings since the war. He left his native Newfoundland twenty-five years earlier to serve in the war-time Royal Navy.

'No, our kid. Am fish room chargehand this trip,' Jack replied. 'I just got fed up of being blown about the deck, thought I'd come indoors for a bit! Any road, what you doin' back. Thought you'd taken Chrimbo off.'

'Yeah, I would've done an' all, if one these thieving bastards hadn't nicked me fucking wallet,' Harry said, pointing his thumb over his shoulder, hitch-hiker style at the others gathered on the whaleback. 'There was all me money in it, three hundred fucking quid.'

'That's rough, Curly.'

'Ah well, carry on regardless, eh?'

Curly Smith was probably the only man Jack knew who could still smile after losing what was half a year's wage for some folk ashore. Harry, an engine room greaser, was known to all as Curly, an ironic nickname due to his cue-ball baldness. He was a natural comic, especially after a couple of pints.

'Hey up, Curly,' said another older crewman proffering his hand. It was Stan Brigham, Curly's near-neighbour and a shipmate of many years. Stan, a fifty-year-old veteran, had also been at sea since he was a lad.

Stan said, 'Did you tell Jack about your wallet?'

'Yeah, Stan,' Jack said. 'He was just saying.'

'Can we talk about summat else, lads?'

'Aye, all right, Curly. You can always cheer us up in t'mess room wi' one o' your turns, eh?' Jack added. Curly was a favourite in the mess room, pub or house party. A few voyages earlier, one of the lads got a great photo of him in the engine room. Curly had taken a length of copper pipe, a trumpet mouthpiece and an old oil funnel and fashioned a bizarre French horn-style instrument with which he then drove his engine room pals mad. But Curly's "top turn" was to strip to the waist, take ashes from the mess room stove, scattering them liberally on the floor, before doing his one-man Wilson, Keppel and Betty sand dance while loudly humming the *Ballet Egyptien*. A tablecloth and a rearrangement of his trademark beret with his neckerchief tucked in the back and a snake belt as headband completed the costume. With his slim build and pencil moustache, Curly had a strong resemblance to the men from the famous British vaudeville act.[7]

The older group of sparehands were joined by Siggy Sigurdssen, a thirty-one-year-old Icelander, whose given name Johan was used only by his wife. Scottish sparehand Jimmy Hamilton, a forty-two-year-old father to five girls and two little boys, joined the Icelander – 'a couple of foreigners together,' Siggy joked. Across the whaleback the young lads from the Maybury pub photo gathered: Tony Harrison, twenty, deckie learner David Young, seventeen, and Kenny Pullen, twenty. They were joined by Tony's pal and neighbour, twenty-one-year-old Eric Petrini, a tall, good-looking lad with a tough-guy reputation. Imagine Buddy Holly without the glasses and that was Eric. Bobby Coulman, nineteen, and twenty-four-year-old Jack Matthews stood with the oldest of that bunch, Jeff "Chuck" O'Dell, a thirty-four-year-old father-of-six, who had been at sea for more than twenty years and was also big pals with Eric. Next alongside was sparehand Paddy Tognola, twenty-six, and his pal Taff Evans, twenty-eight.

Unusually for the rugby league fortress that is Hull, these two men shared a passion for the football team Hull City AFC, and the fortunes and trials of the Tigers took up a lot of the conversation in the mess room and the cabin they shared. Their pal Vic Bull, at twenty-nine, completed the younger part of the crew. A mixture of loudly coloured zoot suits, large quiffs, cowboy shirts and boots, the younger fisher lads stood out from their older, more conservatively dressed shipmates across the whaleback.

From the wheelhouse "All Passengers Ashore" was sounded and the men drifted below decks in small groups. Some of the cabbies who had come aboard for a final drink left sharpish. It would not be the first time a drunk taxi driver had ended up on an Arctic voyage by accident. As the younger members of the crew passed by the older ones, Curly Smith just couldn't help himself.

'Hey up, lads, it's Freddie and the Dreamers!'

"The Dreamers" met Curly's quip with a resounding chorus of 'fuck off'.

The sparehands made for the crew's mess room. Curly went off to join the second engineers George Grinlaw and Trevor Hardwick along with fellow greaser John Scott in the engine room, where chief engineer Williams would give them their orders and sort out their six hours on, six hours off shifts as well as their watch duties.

The engine room of the *St Finbarr* was as much of a temple of modernity as her wireless room. Chief Williams and his men were dwarfed by the massive eight-cylinder direct-injection Hawker Siddeley diesel engine. Engineers develop a relationship with the engines they look after. Williams and his men were no different. It was a joy for them to work in this super-modern powerhouse. Hughie and his men very much had the bragging rights among their mates back in Hull with that much-vaunted engine.

There are a couple of anecdotal theories about the origins of the phrase "steaming drunk". One is that it derived from the old Clyde paddle steamers that took families on river trips from Glasgow out to the Isles of Bute. Licensing laws did not apply to these vessels, so there was many a "da" who took his chance to binge drink his way "doon the watter" to the chagrin of his wife and weans*.

---

* Scots' vernacular for child, particularly in the west of Scotland.

The other is linked to the drinking habits of the fisherman, who made the most of it after the opening of the "Bond" at the start of the outward trip. The outgoing trip is known among trawlermen as "steaming out." Soon, when they reached the fishing grounds, their lives would be the hardest imaginable back-breaking eighteen-hour shifts of fishing and gutting in blood-chilling temperatures, with just six hours' sleep before being at it again. The skin on the hands would blister and burst and crack and bleed and harden as they kept gutting the seemingly endless supply of cold, wet, slippery fish. The salt from the seawater seared into the broken skin. The pain was searing at first until the skin hardened again. Little wonder those who battled each day in the world's most dangerous industry took a drink when they could and eased their lot before the long stint of hard, sober work ahead.

It was quite common to hear trawlermen swear they'd never return to sea, especially after a hard trip. However, circumstances always forced them back – and the booze helped them deal with that necessity.

In the *St Finbarr*'s mess, the men relaxed. They were told which watches they would be in for the voyage. There were three crew watches: the mate's, the bosun's and the third hand's. The engineers, cooks and radio man had their own work schedule.

The skipper had allowed the Bond to be opened. The men chose their cigarettes, booze, chocolates, sweets etc., to go with carry-outs they had brought aboard.

The big cathedral radio provided music for the men at the various Formica-topped tables as they sat smoking, chatting, drinking. Some of the younger guys had small battery-powered portable transistor radios kept for the rare occasions they could listen to them in their cabins. Shelves with cowboy books, thrillers, *True Crime* and the occasional "jazz mags" that the lads had brought back from Norway and Sweden provided the shipboard entertainment.

Opening the Bond could prove dangerous – closing it more so. After all, a dozen or so men already drunk when they arrived on ship don't take kindly to time being called on their steaming-out piss-up. Stories of drunken antics at sea were legion in the bars of Hessle Road, but it was a weak (and therefore poor) skipper who let the men rule the Bond's opening times. Some skippers were immensely strict, others less so, but there were none who would debilitate their crew. On the other hand, sales from the Bond added to the company's profits, so prohibition was out of the question.

Any crewman who had served with Sawyer knew that crossing him was never a good idea. An angry skipper could ruin a man's life by simply putting the word out that he was a bad lot. This form of blacklisting was known as being on "walkabout" – usually a man who had crossed the line would be out of work for a few weeks and learned his lesson.

Others who pissed the skipper off continually could find himself out of work for a long time. The price of a drink gave a trawlerman a lot to think about. Skippers were ultimate autocrats and the men knew it. One famous story that did the rounds that year concerned a sidewinder called the *Ross Cleveland*, owned by rival firm Hudson's and skippered by a man called Philip Gay. Skipper Gay was quite unusual as trawlermen went. He rarely drank and never swore. Many fishermen knew of Gay's catchphrase, 'Stab a sausage!' – which he used when others would turn to automatic obscenity. However, any man who mistook Skipper Phil Gay's eccentricities for weakness would be in for a shock. He was as tough as they came. The story that did the rounds in the early 1960s quickly went into lore.

During one particularly rowdy steaming-out, the men of the *Ross Cleveland* tried a drunken mess room mutiny when Gay called time. One of the men grabbed the key from the commander's hand and threw it to one of his shipmates.

'What you gonna do now, skipper?!' another shouted.

Phil Gay said nothing. He left the mess. The men cheered and one of them liberated some more rum and beer in his absence. The melee continued for ten minutes. Gay returned unnoticed. Then he made his way to the front of the Bond.

'You!' he shouted at the man who had taken the key. 'Give it here. You've got until I count to five.'

'Fuck off.'

The deckhand did not see the right upper-cut coming. The key left his hand and hit the mess deck shortly before he did. The men moved towards their skipper en masse.

'D'you want some of this, lads? Go on, test me. I dare you.'

It was then they noticed the weapon in his hand. He raised it and pointed at the crew. It was the gun used to launch flares – and it was loaded.

'I thought so!' Gay said. He beckoned to a deckhand. 'You… give me that key. Now!'

The men backed off to the tables and took up their playing cards, mumbling among themselves.

'Anything to say, lads?'

The mumbling diminished.

'I didn't think so.'

The laid-out deckhand began to come to.

'And you...' Gay added, as he stepped over the prone, pissed deckhand, 'are gonna be on walkabout 'til you're a greybeard.'[8] So, when mate Collier told the lads the Bond was closing, there was some grumbling, a few last-minute purchases and resignation to make do with the bags of booze they had in their kitbags!

In the *St Finbarr*'s wheelhouse, Sawyer telegraphed the engine room. Below decks George Grinlaw and Curly Smith followed the captain's commands, supervised by chief Williams. The Mirrless engine's torque thundered low as the *St Finbarr* made its way to the lock gates which led to the Humber's wide estuary. Back on the bridge, bosun Samms took the wheel, a position he'd keep until they passed the Spurn Light Ship, off the East Yorkshire coast. Until then Sawyer and the mate would be planning the trip, charting what grounds would be visited and in what order. The *St Finbarr* drew level with the lock keeper's office. From his window the keeper called out, 'Where bound, master?'

'Grand Banks, Newfoundland.' Bosun Samms shouted back from the half-opened wheelhouse window.

CHAPTER FIVE

November 20. Four days out, 200 miles north-northwest of the Pentland Firth.

She should have taken approximately twenty-four hours to reach Pentland Firth, the strait that separates Caithness from the Orkneys, which was her final land sighting before the Grand Banks. Winds ranged from force ten to fourteen. Sawyer felt as if those high winds and churning waves had somehow deliberately followed him from the Humber Estuary. It would be another 2,000 miles or so until land would be seen again. After she left Hull, the *St Finbarr* was forced to crawl through powerful gales and gigantic seas. The skipper could not get a break. It was relentless. From Spurn Point, the weather got harder. For almost sixty hours, the *St Finbarr* prowed almost dead slow, head to wind, climbing huge wave after wave. Up, up, up… then drop.

The crew of any ship near enough saw her rise, disappear, then rise again. The repetitive manoeuvres by Skipper Sawyer ensured not only the safety of his men, but also kept his ship in one piece – ready for when the first trawl would be shot.

Patience and fortitude are as premium to the trawler skipper as courage and experience. In a surging sea, going head to wind is the only way to come through the storm. The ship climbed and fell, her crew felt nervous, some sick, but all knew it was the safest way. It was when the ship moved side to side that men grew fearful. Even in the skilful hands of men like Sawyer, she could be taken in an instant if this was to happen.

Waves of between thirty to sixty feet hit sideways-on made her lay port or starboard, before she straightened up for more of the same. Trawlermen called this "taking a sea." It made hearts jump and stomachs heave.

Sawyer knew he had to maintain the relentless head-to-wind strategy. In good weather the Pentland Firth would have been reached within thirty hours, tops. In the maelstrom Sawyer went slow, sometimes dead slow, to make sure they would reach the fishing grounds intact. Giant waves could easily smash through wheelhouse windows or damage the ship's plates (outer walls), or sweep away deck equipment and any man tending it. While steaming out, men prepared and renewed wires and ensured that the trawl prepared as a courtesy by the previous crew was in working order. They checked life rafts and tested winches that would drag the hopefully bulging nets, the cod-ends of which would release tons of fish, time after time.

Sawyer had also to beware of any change of wind direction, especially with a stern trawler. A sudden switch in a gale would send water up the stern ramp and unbalance the ship. He had to anticipate what might be to the fore, aft, starboard and port to stay safe.

For this, not one man aboard begrudged "that bastard in the cod office" his film-star wages.

Down in the mess room, Old Jack Smith was distracted. He wasn't paying attention to his JT Edson[1]. He held tight on to his tin mug of Camp Coffee, lest it slid. He had just finished his watch. A piece of fried fish and bread lay half-eaten on the plate. A few men were in the mess. A loud 'Oh, fur fuck's sake!' caused Jack to look across to two deckies who seconds earlier had been playing draughts. The board crashed into the two-inch-high ridge around the table top, which was there to stop things flying off. Pieces scattered in various directions like tiny black and white air hockey pucks. The ship listed again. Jack put down his western novel, reached into the shirt pocket under his gansey and took out a small pewter flask. He tipped some of its contents into the tin mug.

The game-playing deckies decided on dominoes. At least if those moved, the game wasn't ruined as quickly. No sooner had the small wooden box touched the table top when it flew out of the deckie's hands. The ship rose on a big wave. The clatter of the white faux-ivory pieces on the Formica top was drowned out by the boom and the whoosh of the trawler as it climbed and dropped. Jack unscrewed the top of the flask that was still in his hand. He tipped it again into the tin mug, the content of which was now roughly forty per cent chicory coffee and sixty per cent Pusser's Rum. Jack knew that this, his first trip on a freezer trawler, would be his last, come what may. He was not the first trawlerman in a gale to come to this conclusion, but Jack had a plan.

He supped from the mug and thought back to chats with his boy before he left. His twenty-two-year-old son Alan was surprised his dad had even decided to go on the *St Finbarr*.

'What the hell do you know about freezers, Dad? You're a sideman, a bosun.'

'What is there to know, kid? I know this much. It'll be my last trip and it won't be spent on a fucking freezing deck, terrified to take a sea, gutting for hours in all bloody weather. I'll be indoors for a change.'

'Oh, come on, how many times have you told us "this is the last trip", Dad? A million?' Alan said.

This time his father's tone was convincing – and he rarely heard the old man swear.

'I know, I know. But I fucking mean it this time, our Alan. I've got a few bob in't bank. I'll do one big last trip and that should get me enough dough.'

'For what?'

'For a pub, that's what.' Jack saw the lad's face start to break into a grin.

'Don't laugh, kid. I'll take you to see it. The Coach and Horses at Patrington. You could be the cook. It would be good for your mam's nerves, being in the countryside. I've just fucking had enough, son. It's time to come ashore.'[2]

Jack drank his tin-mug cocktail and thought back to the bus trip to Patrington in rural East Yorkshire when he and his lad spent hours talking with the publican. It all seemed perfect. He had the savings. The kids could muck in. His Joan could rest up. She had suffered with lung complaints all her life and was in and out of hospital. He had been at sea since he was a kid, served on a minesweeper in the war, been on hundreds of voyages. It was time. It seemed right. He could almost see his name above the door: JOHN SMITH (PROP & LICENCEE). Perfect.

'Water, water, everywhere and still we're on the drink! C'mon Jack, gie's a tot!'

It was Curly Smith. The breath fumes that drifted across the table let the old greaser know there was rum to be had. Curly removed his trademark big white beret and pulled his gansey off over his head, revealing his oil-stained vest. He straightened his sweat rag (neckerchief) and proffered his mug to Jack. He had just finished his six hours below. Jack tipped the flask at Curly's cup.

'You look a bit out o' sorts, our kid. What's up?' Curly said perfunctorily. (It was like when folk say. 'How are you doing?' – they don't want to know.) Curly got more than just a tot as Jack told him his plans for the pub and how this would be the last trip. Curly nodded in the right places and took a few more tots.

To keep his side of the conversation going, he added, 'It's a lot of dough to buy a boozers, Jack.'

'I've got enough put by in't bank,' Jack replied.

'Don't trust banks, me,' Curly decreed.

'Aye, well mebbe if you did, you'd be 300 quid better off and not be getting thrown about the ogin right now, soft lad.'

'Good point,' said Curly draining the tin mug.

'Your boss is here, Curly,' Jack said and nodded towards the door.

Chief Williams' figure filled the frame.

'Hey up, Curly. Come wi' me.'

'But I've just finished, chief.'

'Never mind bloody just finished, get here. There's another bloody short-circuit. Sparks coming from a davit. Get off yer arse, get here and let's get it sorted.'

Jack carried on with his rum. The tin mug had not even the pretence of coffee any more. Jack was drinking more than he had for a long time. It was noticed on his previous ship. Truth was, Jack had lost his nerve. The pub dream was his sincere wish, but it was also his cover story to get ashore. He could never let folk know.

Only a fortnight before he came aboard the *St Finbarr*, Jack had been presented with a bravery award from the Royal Humane Society for rescuing a deckie who was swept overboard, off Flamborough Head. A wave had taken the deckhand over. Quick-thinking Jack got a line and lifebelt to the lad, and he was pulled back on board. Jack had taken a hell of a chance so near the rail, as did the men who came to his aid and helped the terrified kid. They could easily have followed him in. That was in July 1965.[3] The summer. Weather was not supposed to be like that in summer.

Forty-odd years at sea told Jack nothing was ever as it was supposed to be.

Ironically, this heroism had planted the seeds of fear. He had seen how close that deckhand he had saved had come to death. He knew his nerve had gone but he could not admit it. Who was going to feed the family? Jack could not afford the luxury of cowardice. He kept going back. Back to an old sidewinder, the *Southella*.

As bosun he'd be on deck regularly, especially when the nets were hauled or shot out. Unlike the stern freezers, a sidewinder's catch was dropped on the deck to be gutted and then sent to the fish hold. Men worked in all weathers, battered by waves of icy water for shifts of often eighteen hours or more, with their foreman – the bosun – overseeing it all. Trawlermen are hard-drinking men, so when they comment on another's boozing, there's a problem. They know when one of their own has lost it. Sparehands noticed the smell of rum from Jack when on deck and how he flinched when they took a sea. There was no sympathy. Quite the reverse. Jack became the butt of mess room jibes. One of the young deckies on the *Southella*, a kid called Ray Coles, never missed a chance to get his mates to join in ragging the older man. The piss-taking was ruthless and Jack knew he had to either bear it, or fuck off. In the mess, when high waves hit the portholes, or when the ship listed or a giant wave crashed on deck, Coles or one his pals would not be far away with a snide remark.

'Whooo! Jack, that's a big un. Best have another swig, eh?'

The fisher lads never saw this as anything other than ragging, pure and simple. They had been very proud of Jack when he saved that kid. He was a good boss, but he had lost it and he had it coming. Jack left the *Southella*. A few months later she was scrapped. He spent time on a few more sidewinders, including the *Ross Cleveland* under Phil Gay, the skipper famed for the "flare gun incident." Compared to past berths, the *St Finbarr* was like a cruise ship for Jack, but it was not the ships that had gotten to him – it was the sea.[4]

Aft of the wheelhouse, chief Williams and Curly stood in front of the davit that held a full-sized lifeboat. It was dark. The davit was held by a gantry above deck and slightly illuminated by the light from the wheelhouse. Its winch was in darkness. The two men pointed flashlights. The beams criss-crossed as they inspected it.

'What are we looking for, chief?'

'I'm not sure, Curly, but when I was going past earlier there were sparks flying off the davit. I have seen it a few times before but this was the worst yet,' the engineer explained. He went on, 'We were getting thrown about a bit at the time and the sparks coming off it were like a kiddie's sparkler going off. A great big kiddie's sparkler at that.'

As Williams spoke, the ship rose and fell sharply – not as powerfully as before – but still with considerable force. Sparks flew from the davit and cascaded a foot or so into the air, then extinguished into the pitch backdrop of the inky night sky as quickly as they appeared. The fire show repeated itself a couple times more as the trawler steadied.

'Like that!' Williams said and pointed at the impromptu pyrotechnics.

Curly moved close to the davit.

'Don't touch!' Williams shouted and grabbed the greaser by his sleeve. 'It's probably live. Shine the torch on it again, Curly.'

The greaser pointed the flashlight and his boss moved closer. At an arm's length, Williams reached and touched the metal with the back of his hand. He was instantly pushed back by the shock. (Electricians never touch any potential electrical source with anything other than the back of hand if forced. This ensures the shock does not "pull them in" and electrocute them.)

'It's live all right, Curly. There's nowt we can do now. Best leave it to morning. Tell the men to stay clear though, especially if she's moving about too much. Something must be loose and earthing wrong when the ship's shifting about in these winds. It's one thing after another. Dave Redshaw was right. The electrics are fucked on this ship. You best get back to the mess, Curly, and take your break. I'm going to take this up with the old man. Again.'

Both men walked toward the wheelhouse. Williams headed for the bridge and Curly went onward, intent to check if old Jack had any rum left. Curly was sure he would. The greaser lingered near the wheelhouse and earwigged to Sawyer and Williams' shouting match before heading below.[5]

Back in the mess, Jack was pleased to see his old pal back at the table, even if it was going to cost him the remainder of his Pusser's Rum. There were a few more men off shift now and the ship had settled. It was still high winds and a swell, but the *St Finbarr* was picking up speed. Lost time was being made up. A few of the lads were playing cards, straining to hear the radio battling the atmospherics that crackled through the speakers. Some were taking advantage of downtime to eat as much as they could in as short a space.

Curly told Jack about what he had overheard from the wheelhouse.

'The chief was giving it loads, Jack, telling him how pissed off he was making-do-and-mend wi' the electrics – and he's got a point. I'm telling you it was Guy Fawkes' Night out there, pal. I mean, Jack, how many little fires and that have we had since this ship's been going out?'

'Couldn't tell you, pal,' Jack replied. 'It's me first trip, innit?'

'Well, I'll tell you, our kid, it's bloody more than enough. And the old man just keeps saying it was all right and passed muster before we left. Electrics have never been right since the maiden trip. It's only fish that he cares about, nowt else!' Curly said.

'I'll tell you summat, though,' one of the deckies piped in, 'if there'd been owt wrong wi' fish room or the freezer, that bastard in't cod office would have it fixed in a flash, pal.'

The crew just wanted to be fishing. The Grand Banks could not come soon enough. It would take their minds off electrics, slow, punishing weather, high winds and big waves.

The promise of big catches and big money would focus the minds of the men of *St Finbarr*.

Newfoundland coast, November 30, 1966, St Andrew's Day
(the patron saint of fishermen).

The trawler looked like a giant, shuddering version of an Admiralty chart silhouette as she passed the iceberg that dwarfed her as she struggled in high winds. The huge terrible beauty was just another obstacle for the beleaguered skipper. These ice behemoths were legion. The only folk that wanted to see them were the binocular-wielding tourists on the coast. The men of *St Finbarr* were in wild waters.

The sea was like slush, so much so that the waves made noise when they hit the ship. It was fourteen days since they had left Hull.

They should have been here in six, but the constant northwest winds more than halved their progress.

However, the fishermen's patron saint had blessed them – with help from Skipper Sawyer. Despite gales, sea swells, ice and delays in getting to the Grand Banks, the catches were as big as ever.

The skipper's uncanny fish-finding skills proved spot-on, as always. The crew of the super-modern factory ship were kept busy round the clock, gutting, freezing and stacking giant haul after giant haul.

The hold was filling up with hundreds of frozen blocks of fish. There were tons of cod, haddock, giant halibut and even large amounts of mackerel (a highly calorific fatty fish favoured by the Russian market). This trip was going to be a big earner.

One hundred miles off Newfoundland the *St Finbarr* took her place in a timeline going back at least five centuries since John Cabot had claimed his "new found lands" for his adoptive king, Henry VII. Giovanni Caboto, a Genovese like his compatriot Columbus, received the patronage of a foreign power, in his case England. His anglicised name was feted in his adopted country. It was reported from his voyage in 1497 that the Italian explorer's crew aboard *The Matthew* caught huge amounts of cod to enhance their harsh seaboard diet. They simply dipped baskets into the water and pulled them out full of fish. Good old Henry VII was so pleased with John Cabot's discoveries that he paid him a princely ten pounds, equivalent to two years' wages for a journeyman in trade. Had he brought home spices rather than salted fish this would have much more! Cabot's voyage of discovery from Bristol to the Grand Banks was reckoned to be the first to bring Europeans to that part of the American continent since the Vikings. By the seventeenth century, French and English fishermen began to spend winters in Newfoundland and, although French residents were forced to leave in the 1700s, a French migrant fishery continued along the northern part of the island.

English-speaking Newfoundlanders had largely replaced the migrant fishers inshore by about 1815. The fish stocks became important for the early economies of eastern Canada and the United States schooners based in New England, and Newfoundland began to make inroads on the Europeans' share of the catch.[6] Many things had changed since the times of Cabot but the landscape and dangers of these ancient bountiful fishing grounds had not. Icebergs the size of cathedrals, quick-freezing waters in giant patches of low salinity, combined with the fierce unpredictable climate and the blinding fogs that dropped suddenly, when the warmth of the Gulf Stream crossed with local cold currents.

The sea has a landscape and terrain as the land does. The Grand Banks is a large area of submerged highlands southeast of Newfoundland and east of the Laurentian Channel on the North American continental shelf. It covers 36,000 square miles. The banks are relatively shallow, ranging from eighty to 330 feet (twenty-five to 100 metres) deep. Here the cold Labrador Current mixes with the warm waters of the Gulf Stream. This mixing and the shape of the ocean bottom lifted nutrients to the surface and created one of the richest fishing grounds in the world. It became important to both the Canadian and the high seas fisheries, with fishermen across the centuries risking their lives among rogue waves, fog, icebergs, sea ice, hurricanes, nor'easter winter storms and even earthquakes. (A major eruption in 1929, known as the Grand Banks Earthquake, on the southwest bordering the Laurentian Channel in November of that year, caused an underwater landslide; it resulted in extensive damage to transatlantic cables and generated a rare Atlantic tsunami that hit the south coast of Newfoundland and eastern Cape Breton Island, claiming twenty-seven lives in the Burin Peninsula.) This was the world's most important international fishing area in the nineteenth and early twentieth centuries. The next big fishing ground after the Grand Banks, the Flemish Cap, is a wild, hurricane-strewn 17,000 square mile stretch of sea, with depths of 1,500 metres and more; home to cod, plaice, halibut, redfish and a booming shrimp fishery.

A modern layman's vision of fishing is perhaps the biblical vista of "men of Galilee" casting nets and hauling by hand. The crew of the super-ship *St Finbarr* that winter could not have been further from that. Each trawl was a huge concern, shot from the stern. The warps, massive long thick wires attached to chains with links a foot in circumference, would be roughly three times as long as the depth being fished. In this instance, these would be at least 1,000ft long. The parallel warp lines led to "otter doors" – weighing a ton each – connected by further lines to giant bobbins known as Dan Lenos which ensured the eighty-feet-wide mouth of the net stayed wide open. A 200ft-long net would be dragged like a massive stocking pulled through the depths. The whole rig was dragged more than a mile behind the ship. Immense, loud rattling of chains that rumbled down the stern ramp as the trawl was shot drowned all other noise, even the great engines. It felt as if the very rivets were being shaken out of the ship's plates.

Men supervising it all communicated in sign as unprotected ears were assailed by industrial-scale cacophony. They knew their jobs inside-out. They had to. Error was costly – often fatal. Winches that shot the trawl were powered by the Hawker Siddeley deck engine. Below in the engine room, instruments showed the variances in torque (like the rev counter does in a car). When the trawl got heavier, torque dropped. A sudden decrease or increase indicated a potential disaster; the former could be a break in the lines – and the latter a jamming of the net on a rock or other undersea obstacles that could put paid to thousands of pounds worth of gear and fish.

From the wheelhouse to the stern ramp, engine room to winch, observation was paramount. Once the trawl was shot, that ramp was upped and secured as quickly as possible. Water taken on too quickly or in too much volume meant catastrophe could soon follow with the potential destabilisation of the vessel.

At hauling in, the winches and the wires and chains on the aft gantries would drag the huge bulging net with between two to three tons of fish up the stern ramp. It would be lifted above the open trap that led to the factory deck. The cod end would burst open and the fish would cascade like thousands of silver bullion bars falling from the sky. In the factory deck below the crews would be ready to gut and press the fish into fast-frozen blocks of about three feet square, each one dropped through a trapdoor gap like a giant postbox opening. These frozen blocks would then be stored alternately port and starboard of the hold, ensuring the ship's balance. As that work went on, another trawl was under way, ensuring eighteen-hour shifts for the changing crews, whose six hours off would be spent eating and sleeping, ready for the same again, and again and again.

Each trawl on average would be three or four hours. Every sharp-bladed knife that cut into a haddock belly, each cod liver thrown to the process bin, the swift and efficient expulsion of guts and fish debris via the vacuum pipes into the ocean, saw bulging pay packets in the minds of the crew get ever fatter with each gutted fish. [7]

Skipper Sawyer was doing what he did best – filling fish holds.

Next day, the first of December, the weather was still rough, but more manageable. High swells lifted and dropped the ship, but the fishing was improving and so was Skipper Sawyer's mood. The *St Finbarr* was on its way to another bumper catch. They had certainly made up for time wasted. In the mess room a small cinema screen was put up and a projector brought in. The men not working or on watch were in for a treat. Cowboy films. Trawlermen loved the cowboy movies. Maybe because they kind of saw themselves in that pioneer role, kings of the wild frontiers of the sea. The young fisher lads' dress ashore, cowboy boots to match their Nashville-style shirts coupled with love of all things country and western, reinforced this. Skipper Sawyer was no different. He did not dress like a fisher lad any more but he was still one at heart, like all his colleagues. And he loved the cowboy pictures too.

There were no "accelerated promotion schemes" for the trawlerman. Every skipper started at the bottom as a deckie learner – which is why even the toughest, meanest bastards to grace a wheelhouse got respect, if not always admiration. The men knew he had done everything he would ever ask them to do – and sometimes more. Behaviour in the mess room was a bit calmer than usual as the old man had joined the audience. The lights went down. The projector whirred into life. The fluttering, twitching smoke-filled beams worked their magic. The men reverted to a second childhood and cheered, stamped and whistled like the kids at a Saturday morning ABC Minors show as Randolph Scott's name loomed large above the title. But the bad guy had barely ridden into Dead Man's Gulch when the picture faded and died. The sound went as the power failed and it mimicked the noise that *Lost in Space*'s Robbie the Robot made when suddenly switched off. Only the deckhead lights stayed on. Amid boos and jeers, one of the deckies said, 'Fucking fuse's blown!' Sawyer left the dimly lit mess, promising the crew he would be back and would fix the fault. He headed back to the wheelhouse.

Hughie Williams was in the engine room. The horse-shoe-shaped corridor around it housed the crew's accommodation. The doorways to the engine room were from both port and starboard and led to the same corridor. For a brief second Hughie noticed the lights outside flickered. He caught it in the corner of his eye. When he looked out the lights were working fine. The steady thrum of the engine and the almost rhythmic rising and falling of the ship provided the background noise for chief Williams and second engineer Trevor Hardwick. Hughie looked out again. He was certain he saw the lights flicker this time.

'Another bloody fuse or earth fault, Trevor. It's beyond a joke.'

The second engineer did not reply. He was looking in the opposite direction.

'Look, chief… smoke!'

Both engineers grabbed anti-smoke masks from the hooks on the wall and ventured into the corridor. The smoke was not overpowering but it was gathering momentum. Within minutes the men were outside the cabin door, Hardwick with a fire extinguisher in hand. Smoke came out from under it. Given that the doors were sealed tight to the frame, this indicated there must be a strong fire inside. Williams tried the handle.

'It's locked. I'll get the key.' Williams ran to the wheelhouse, leaving his colleague in the corridor as the smoke began to billow thicker. Within minutes Williams was back. The door was opened and the smoke engulfed both men. They strained to see but soon figured the source was the wardrobe near the bottom bunk. They pulled open that door. Inside a cardboard box full of beer bottles was ablaze, as was the inside of the wardrobe. Hardwick put out the fire within seconds. The smoke cleared and the men saw the fire's source. The cabling to the light above the bottom bunk near the wardrobe was chafed and burned. The men repaired the cable as best they could.

'You should report this to the old man, chief,' said Hardwick.

Williams shot back an irritated glance.

'Yeah, he could put it in the fire drill book and then ignore it.'

Williams left Hardwick to finish the repairs. The chief returned the key to Sawyer without a word being exchanged. There was no point. Sawyer left the wheelhouse and Williams followed. The skipper headed for the mess room. The engineer went back to his engines. He resumed his work with second engineer Hardwick. A cheer went up from the mess room. There was some stamping and whistling.

'Looks like they've got the projector working,' quipped Hardwick.

They both laughed. What else could they do?[8]

Later back in his cabin, chief Williams was reading by the lamp in his bunk. He put the book down and looked closer at the tape-bound light fitting overhead.

'Another half-arsed botch job,' thought Williams. He switched off the lamp. He was in no mood for reading. The dog-tired engineer drifted off into a fitful sleep. He had only been asleep five minutes when he was awakened by a rapping on his cabin door. It opened and there was Harry Prince with a tea-tray in hand.

'Thought you might want a cuppa, chief?'

'Aye, grand, come in, Harry. Sit down.'

The cook sat on the chair next to the chief's desk and poured out some tea.

'Would you like a little summat in it?'

Harry poured the rum into the mug from the flask he took from his pocket before Hughie could answer either way. The man that powered the ship and the man that powered the crew drank together and made small talk. A few minutes later, Harry said, 'I'm off up to the cod office now to take them a brew.'

'Aye, grand, Harry. See you later.'

The two men nodded a goodnight. The cook headed for the skipper's cabin with the tea-tray and the chief drifted back to fitful sleep. The two men, although not great friends, always made time to chat when they met, especially on board. For Harry – like the chief – had also survived a sinking. Such men were known throughout the community – being a survivor had a kind of minor celebrity status. Given the superstitious nature of the trawlerman, such men were welcomed aboard, on the premise that lightning did not strike twice, did it?

The sinking that Harry survived proved him an incredibly lucky man indeed as it was caused by the incompetence of two skippers, on calm waters in midsummer.

It was coincidentally on another Hamling ship, the *St Celestin* – so Harry had more reasons than most to be choosy about the commanders with whom he sailed. On May 27, 1957, the *St Celestin* sank after a 'very avoidable collision' with Boyd Line trawler *Arctic Viking*. Both had been sailing too close to one another. The *Arctic Viking*'s nets were out at the time but the skipper of the *St Celestin* did not notice until both ships were almost upon each other. Both the *St Celestin*'s skipper Percy May and that of the *Arctic Viking* Robert Gray had issued short whistle blasts to warn the other to stop. However, neither skipper properly heeded the other and the *Arctic Viking* had to cut her nets as she crashed stern first into the starboard side of the *St Celestin*. That ship began to sink.

The lifeboat on the starboard side was inaccessible and the crew of twenty, including the skipper, abandoned ship on two life rafts launched with just minutes to spare. All the men were saved and taken aboard the *Arctic Viking*.

A Court of Inquiry hearing held in Hull in July that year, led by Judge Waldo Porges, heard that a series of catastrophic mistakes were made by both commanders. The court was told that both men had been alone on their respective bridges at the time of the crash. No explanation was given to the court for this.

The inquiry heard how the *St Celestin* was heading south, about fifty miles off Bear Island, when her skipper first noted the *Arctic Viking* some three or four miles away. May's ship was intending to trawl a 160-fathom patch nearby. It was about seven in the evening; visibility was good and the sea was moderate. There was no reason Skipper May should have not been able to stay clear of the other trawler which was going southwesterly. May could now see that the *Viking* was fishing even though she was not exhibiting the regulation basket, the universally accepted signal that a trawl was shot.

In summing up, Judge Porges said, 'Shortly afterwards, he (May) saw the *Arctic Viking* coming round on to a southerly heading on which she appeared steady for only a few seconds. She was then four cables (roughly 800 yards) away and still bearing about four points on the starboard bow of the *St Celestin*. The skipper of the *St Celestin* said that he then realised that he should give the *Arctic Viking* a good clearance but took no action at that stage.' The judge added that it was only when the *Arctic Viking* was roughly 400 yards away that May tried to take avoiding action. But it was too late. Both ships simultaneously blasted steam whistles, but the *Arctic Viking* had swung to port to take a bow wave. Although she kept heading towards the *St Celestin*, Skipper May still took no avoiding action. It was just forty-five seconds from then that the *St Celestin*'s engine room was ordered "full speed astern". Then the 533-ton *Arctic Viking* crashed stern first into the starboard side of the 790-ton *St Celestin*, which sank very shortly afterwards, leaving her crew in two life rafts to be rescued by the surviving trawler. It was at the end of that hearing that Judge Porges urged all trawlers to keep new-style life rafts aboard and train the men in their use. The industry paid heed. By 1966, all shipping carried them. In fact, they were much more effective over the years than the lifeboat, which many trawlermen and sailors felt was a throwback to the days of Captain Bligh and kept the old guard at the Board of Trade comfortable. Judge Porges said, 'These appliances clearly proved their worth in the circumstances of this casualty, one of the most apparent advantages being the ease with which they were employed. Had those rafts not been available this collision might well have resulted in serious loss of life.' Both skippers were banned from working for a year.[9] Ever since, Harry always felt safer knowing the life rafts were there to complement the lifeboat. It was always the first thing he checked when aboard. It was good practice, especially on the *St Finbarr*, given the state of her lifeboat's electrified davits.

In the wheelhouse, mate Collier signed the fire drill book. It showed the men had been successfully put through their paces. Nothing to report. There never was. For each drill completed there was a small entry, signed by him and counter-signed by Sawyer. When he had put his moniker next to that day's report, he handed the leather-bound book back to the boss. Sawyer smiled.

'Another perfect drill, mate. Well done. Especially given it's blowing a gale out.' The skipper laughed as he signed and put the book back in its drawer for another fortnight. Collier smiled back uncomfortably and left the bridge. Sawyer went back to his charts. Bosun Samms was at the wheel concentrating dead ahead.

The owners' health and safety rules were clear. For every fourteen days at sea the crew of the *St Finbarr* would do a fire drill. The officer conducting it would report to the mate for his signature as proof the procedure had been carried out properly. If any issues came up they would be reported to Hull and recorded in the book.

According to the *St Finbarr*'s book, she was an exemplar – all ship-shape and Bristol fashion – a surprise to the crew given the amount of light failures, small fires and earth-wire problems reported in previous trips, especially those highlighted by the previous radio man that had led to the ship being delayed three times before leaving Hull. But the crew had no reason to think it odd. For the reason for the exemplary fire drill record was simple. The book had never left the wheelhouse. The drills never happened. Sawyer thought them a waste of time – and time was money. He was days behind schedule too. A simple solution was put in place. The mate would sign the book each fortnight and that would keep the bosses happy. Sawyer did not think it worth his while to tell the crew. They were there to catch fish and anything that got in the way of that was of no use to him. For him, the fire drills were just paper exercises.

That's what the skipper wanted – and the skipper was God. If the crew did know about it, no one would never dream of complaining, unless they wanted to find themselves on the wrong side of a "walkabout" – a sanction they knew the old man would use in a heartbeat.[10]

Next day, more than 2,000 miles away, a pretty young mum with a baby girl in a pushchair finally got to the post office counter. It was busy on Hessle Road, with hundreds of housewives returning from the owners' offices in West Dock Avenue where they had collected that week's wage. The weekly rush of mums and kids and pushchairs to pick up the men's wages was known locally as the Pram Race. Despite the queue the excited young mum was determined to wait. She had been to her GP before going to pick up her man's money from the Hamlings office. Now she had a telegram to send. After what seemed an age the pretty young housewife got to the front and dictated it. Minutes later the woman behind the counter totted up the words and calculated the cost.

'How would you like it signing then, Mrs Harrison?'

'Jillian, please… Jillian with a "J".'[11]

CHAPTER SIX

Christmas Eve, 1966. One hundred miles off the Labrador coast – 1630hours

Trawlermen call it a "confused sea." Sudden swells lifted the ship then dropped her as quickly as she rose. Waves repeatedly deluged her decks and force ten to fourteen gales randomly changed direction. In the factory decks below, the previous haul was being gutted and frozen. A team of four gutted the catch and a further two ensured the fish were frozen in blocks then stored in the hold. A small thing like atrocious weather did not daunt skipper Sawyer.

On the trawling deck, bosun Samms and his men watched as thundering chains clattered down the stern ramp and followed the huge net, with its 1,000ft of wires and warps, down fifty fathoms with the mile-long trawl. The trawl was shot again. A few hours later another shift in the factory decks would be there for the tons of fish that would finish as frozen blocks and be added to the *St Finbarr*'s fast-filling hold.

In the engine room torque was monitored to keep it all steady and chief Williams obeyed the instructions sent from the brass-handled telegraph in the wheelhouse.

The trawl had been out for about an hour when Williams and his skipper realised simultaneously something was wrong. The fishing would always be stopped when the net was snagged, putting the ship in immediate danger. In the engine room Williams noticed the revs race as the ship pulled against an increasingly immobile object. The skipper did not need the engine room to tell him what was happening. Somewhere approximately a mile from the vessel, between thirty to fifty fathoms under the raging Grand Banks, the net was caught.

It could be anything from a rock on the seabed to a submarine. Neither Sawyer nor his chief engineer took the time to consider. The priority was to get the net gear hauled in as quickly and as safely as possible. Not only was it urgent for safety but also for the economics of the trip. Lost gear cost thousands of pounds to replace, as would the fish trapped in the damaged nets. This was another example of the constant line between profit and safety that a skipper and his crew walked daily. Snagging like this could happen at any time.

The ship's irregular motion in the confused sea did not help the men who manned the winches, and those astern, there to retrieve it.

For once in this cursed trip there was some luck. Sawyer caught a break – literally. The gear loosened off from whatever had caught it. An hour later, the part-haul from damaged nets was being processed. Whatever it was had given way, but there could be no more fishing until repairs were done.

Sawyer ordered sparehand/chargehand Paddy Tognola to head up the repairs. With him were Tony Harrison, Eric Petrini, Chuck O'Dell and Taff Evans. The repair would be a long job.

The lads liked Petrini. He had a reputation as a joker, the sort who helped the time pass quicker even with the most arduous tasks. Deckies were always pleased to see him on the factory deck. Where work is hard, the humour is usually good. Work was always hard for the men of the *St Finbarr*. These men were all mates ashore too. So, the daunting task would at least feel slightly less of a chore.

The lads were about half an hour into the job when the sparks, Tommy Gray, came over. In his hand was a pile of papers. It was the Christmas telegrams from back home. Tony Harrison seemed more keen than the others to get to Gray.

'Steady on, mate. There's no money in them,' one of the lads quipped.

The men took an impromptu break to scan the news from home, the precious Marconigrams from Hull with messages from the wives and bairns for whom they risked their lives as sea.

Petrini whipped out a pocket flask and passed it to his mate Tony Harrison.

'Cheers, pal!' Petrini said.

Tony took a swig and managed to get the flask back to his shipmate just in time.

Sawyer came on to the deck.

'How long, Paddy?'

Tognola replied, 'It'll be as quick as it is, skipper.'

'Well, make sure it's as quick as possible. We've got a hold to fill.'

'We'll do our best.'

'You will that. I want the next trawl before midnight, so get about it, lads.'

Sawyer turned sharply and headed back to the wheelhouse. When he was far enough away, one of the deckies said, 'Hey lads, we won't have time put our Christmas stockings up!'

'The only stocking he'll want hanging on Christmas morning will be that big one over the back of the boat,' Petrini quipped.

The lads laughed and Eric added in mock anger, 'Hey up, not too loud. He might think we're enjoying ourselves!'

It was freezing and the men's hands stung in the bitter cold under their mittens as they set about mending the trawl. It was minus ten degrees Celsius. (It was what trawlermen called '"piss on your hands" weather. Legions of deckie learners down the ages learned the benefit of this unsavoury practice early in their careers. Old salts believed it not only warmed the hands but also helped heal the numerous searing cuts and burst blisters suffered, especially by new deckies.)

The low salt content of the seawater meant it was part-frozen in massive patches and some waves had the consistency of slush. Luckily, the ship had not iced up to an unmanageable level. Ice is the biggest natural enemy of the trawler. Any build-up on the wires or rails must be constantly chipped off. If a ship was icing rapidly, it was not unusual for the skipper to assign every man bar the engineers to ice-breaking duty. They would use picks, spanners, shovels and even marlin spikes to rid the ship of a potentially fatal build-up.

It takes only twenty tons of ice on the superstructure to make a ship "turn turtle" – which is when the vessel is turned upside down in seconds and sunk. That's the one thing stern ships and sidewinders had in common.

Sawyer's seamanship, manoeuvres and forcing of crewmen to constantly keep on top of the problem ensured the trawlerman's worst naturally occurring enemy did not send them to their doom. He – like all Hull skippers of his generation – carried with him a lesson seared into the brain, thanks to naval instructor Captain Peter Harvey of the Hull Nautical College. It was Harvey's job to get the men in his charge through their skippers' tickets. The ex-Royal Navy man was an eccentric teacher who was always heeded. His background with the Hessle Amateur Dramatic Society aided the delivery of his lessons. His talk on the dangers of ice was always at the end of the course. Harvey used a scale model of the Hull trawler *D.B. Finn*, in a float tank; on it he placed weights of varying sizes on different parts of the model's superstructure. When he placed the final weight, he took a ladle of water and with his trademark theatrical flourish said, 'Gentlemen… this is your ship!' With that, he tipped the ladle's contents on to the model's deck. The small ship immediately turned turtle. Of all the training at the Hull Nautical College, this was the lesson no man forgot.[1]

Tognola and his team were well into their work. It was still freezing and blowing hard. From time to time the light on the lifeboat davit sent sparks flying into the dark, like an intermittent Roman candle.

'I thought that boat would be fixed by now,' said one of the deckies.

'Yeah, and here's one of the bright sparks that should've sorted it,' replied another. It was greaser Curly Smith walking Charlie Chaplin-style to steady himself against the motion of the ship. He was in a full rubber duck suit complete with sou'wester. In his gloved hands, he had his toolbox in one and a powerful flashlight in the other.

'Hey up, Curly, are you off to fix the davit – again?'

Curly looked up and smiled at the team as they worked.

'No, but you're not gonna believe this, lads. I am only going to fix the lights in the wheelhouse. The old man reported the light outside his door has cut out. What we need is a proper leccy man. It's all botch-up and make do and mend around here.

'I've just been down to see the fuse box with Taff Evans and John Scott before being sent out here – and there's stuff from the last trip that ain't been fixed yet.[2] Seems every time the ship lurches there's a short or fuse blows. It's ridiculous.'

Christmas Day, 0100hours.

Gales lashed the churning mass of waves. Sawyer was alone at his helm. He sent mate Walter Collier to tell the crew there would be no more fishing for now. He decided to give it a few hours before trying again. From the radios in the wireless room and those on the bridge there was a crackling cacophony. Yankee yuletide music from the American Forces Network faded in and out of range amid atmospheric disturbance.

The sets – UHF and VHF – emitted messages in many languages. Radio traffic buzzed across a darkness that only a man of the sea knows. Crews of Russian tankers, US carriers, British merchant vessels and the fishing fleets of many nations, scattered across 50,000 square miles, received Christmas messages from anxious wives and kids and mothers and other loved ones from hundreds of homes across the globe, all in different stages of Christmas Day.

Amid the harsh weather and swirling swells there was a certain peace for the skipper, alone at his command with a Babel of the airwaves – and a glass of Scotch for company. The whisky aided his keen control of his rising and falling ship. Sawyer saw an occasional twinkle of lights come and go. The nearest vessel was at least five miles away.

He could see distant lights more clearly from his "clear view window" – the large disc inset in two of the wheelhouse panes. They spun constantly like a sideways-on record, allowing a constant clearer view. His vision was impaired through ordinary windows, and sheets of wave water made looking through them like trying to see through panes made from sheet ice.

From earlier chats on the VHF he knew that his friend Eddie Wooldridge, skipper of the Hull ship *Orsino*, was on a maiden voyage with the new stern trawler, which had been recently launched in competition to Sawyer's command. The *Orsino* had just arrived in the Labrador water twenty-fours earlier.

At least the *St Finbarr* skipper knew that Wooldridge would not be fishing either in that storm. He was correct. The *Orsino* had laid-to after only one trawl. Sawyer had his ship laid-to also and planned to shoot his trawl again, after he had weathered the storm. The constant thrum from the engine room was felt through the soles of his suede shoes. The crew's accommodation surrounded that engine room below in a U-shaped corridor. Both were over the machinery space.

There was accommodation for twenty-one ratings, up to three to a cabin, together with the galley, crew mess room, provisions and cold store. Above that was the accommodation for the seven officers, including the skipper, the bond store and two cabins usually occupied by boffins from the White Fish Authority, there to collect research data. As this was a Christmas voyage, those men were not there. Crew could get on to the deck from four exits and via either side of the engine room. Mate Collier had told the men to go to their cabins and get some rest and that they might be fishing again at 0230hours. This was wishful thinking on the skipper's part. The storm showed no sign of abating. On the bright side, the ice was under control. It was difficult to think this was the case in the ship's corridors as the high-pressure ventilation, a kind of super-air-conditioning to keep the fish in top condition, gave a chill factor that reached the bone marrow of even the heaviest-clad man. The icy air was blown twenty-four hours a day.

At just before 0230hours, Sawyer ordered that the mended gear be shot but it never left the deck. The swirling sea worried the skipper more than the powerful north-westerly. There was a failure with the hydraulics system that meant he had to revert to manual steering. It was a tough time just keeping the ship steady. He was not a man to give in easily and it was 0400hours when the trawl was finally stowed. Sawyer admitted defeat – for now.

Collier was back on the bridge with the skipper. Sawyer offered him a dram and he took it gratefully in his newly ungloved hand.

'Merry Christmas,' said Sawyer, raising his glass.

'Aye, skipper, Merry Christmas. Cheers.'

Another voice added, 'Merry Christmas to you too, skipper.'

It was followed by a distinctive Scottish accent, 'Aye, all the best there, skipper, from me an a'.'

Sawyer looked up and saw Paddy Tognola and Jimmy Hamilton.

'Jimmy, Paddy, will you have a dram with us?'

The lads did not need to be asked twice.

'Good job with the gear, Paddy, by the way,' the skipper added.

Sawyer then turned to Collier and said, 'Look, we're not going to be hauling owt now. Take the lads a few bottles of beer. And give them a nip from these too,' he added, handing Collier two bottles of Scotch, one of which was half-empty. Tognola and Collier left together for the mess room to dish out the booze. As they left, Sawyer said to Collier, 'Mind now, not too much. Just a sneck lifter.'

Some went to their cabins with the beer and the drams, others stayed in the mess. Season's greetings were exchanged, hands of cards dealt. Tony Harrison and Eric Petrini talked about wives and kids and home and what they would spend in Rayner's when they got there. The two were laughing and joking, and a few more joined them with talk of Christmas telegrams and missing home, and how they'd sink a stack at Rayner's with their film-star wages. The cross-talk was interrupted by a Tannoy announcement.

It crackled into life with the Sawyer's voice announcing, 'Attention all crew…' That opening line was met by a chorus of "fuckin' hells" – and, before the next part of the message, one of the lads said, 'He's not getting out again in this, is he? It's Christmas fucking Day.'

Sawyer's voice went on, 'Merry Christmas, lads. Seeing as it's Christmas Day, those of you who'd like to can join me, the mate and the chief for a dram on the bridge. That is all.' Back in the wheelhouse the faux-exaggerated cheer heard faintly by the skipper told him his message had been heard loud and clear. Most of the crew took up the offer of drinks with the boss. Some of the older men had gone to their cabins. The chance of an extra couple of hours' sleep was Christmas present enough for them. The men on the bridge only stayed about half an hour. After a few yuletide pleasantries and a dram, they found themselves wanting to be elsewhere. As much as they appreciated his hospitality, they had little to say to each other. The rise of a stronger wind was welcomed.

The swell grew and the ship began to roll. Sawyer said, 'Right lads, that's it, I think. This swell's gonna get worse before it wears out. So, you all best get to your cabins, turn in and try to get some kip.'[3] By 0430hours, the ship was rolling and reeling. Below deck the men not on watch slept in spite of the storm, dog-tired and anaesthetised by the "sneck lifter" the skipper had given them. They slept on as their "cradles" rocked.

Once the lights were out in these small cabins, a deep darkness that could not be replicated elsewhere engulfed them. A glow from a roll-up lit by a crewman shone like a flashlight in it.

Above, Skipper Sawyer rallied himself to keep all safe. Sawyer would need all his wits about him. More than 400 tons of fish, 1,139 tons of trawler and twenty-five souls depended on him continually getting it right.

CHAPTER SEVEN

0730hours, Christmas Day, Sunday, December 25.

Sawyer had been awake for more than eighteen hours. The ship was laid starboard-side-to in a gale. It was a northeasterly now. The sea state was still confused and it see-sawed the *St Finbarr*. It was minus ten Celsius. High winds made it feel colder. She was about fifty-five degrees, fifteen minutes north and at a longitude of about fifty degrees and forty-five minutes west, 100 miles off the Labrador coast.[1] Engines maintained constant revs with no pitch on the propeller. Sawyer's diligence had kept his crew and ship safe through the night. This long storm was still to be weathered. It was dark and would be for hours more.

Watch duties were changing and Sawyer would be able to rest soon and hoped to return refreshed later to a ship back at work. They were due back to Hull in fewer than ten days. The hold was three-quarters full, despite the constant maelstroms that had dogged them since they left the Pentland Firth in their wake thirty-eight days earlier. A lull in the weather could mean another record catch, and, more importantly, another record payday. It was also possible that they would be back early to spend it.

Curly Smith was due on watch to replace second cook Dave Whittaker. The cook's patience was wearing thin with the old greaser. Ten minutes had passed since he had been outside the old fella's cabin telling him to get to the mess for breakfast before his duties began.

'Yeah, yeah, Dave lad, I'll be right there.'

'Well, make sure you are, you old get!'

'Merry Christmas to you too, shipmate!' Whittaker was back at Curly's cabin minutes later when he proved a no-show for breakfast. This time Dave held the door wide open. At least the lights were on inside now and the old bugger was not having a swift smoke.

'C'mon Curly, don't take the piss! Get yersen out of your pit.' The old fella surprised the cook with his leap from the upper bunk. He was in his vest and trousers. He pulled on his shoes and grabbed his big white beret then quickly followed Whittaker into the corridor to head for the mess room. His gansey was wrapped around his shoulders. The cabin door was left open.

Just two cabins away, Paddy Tognola slept soundly – exceptionally so for a man in a ship thrown about for days like a tiny sponge in a gigantic freezing slushy Jacuzzi. That is what an eighteen-hour shift, finished off with a couple of drinks, will do to a man.

He slept the sleep of the just worn-out.

In the deckhead, behind the light fittings the smoke built up as it had done for some hours now. It emitted a petro-leum smell, but given how near the accommodation was to the engine room no-one detected it. How could they? Melting wires burned slow and gas forced its way out from the vents. An empty cabin filled with smoke and fumes, again unnoticed. The constant air-conditioning helped it on its way.

Paddy's deep sleep became a struggle for life. He could not breathe. Thick smoke that tasted of oil filled his mouth and forced its way to his lungs. He threw himself from his bunk. He tried to shout to his mates. All-enveloping darkness disorientated him. It was like there was a dark hand over his face that pushed his mouth and nose closed while his throat was choked with smoke the consistency of spiky candyfloss. It was killing him in the deep, deep dark. He panicked and grabbed at the light switch. Nothing. He managed to get to the door and opened it. A rush of cold air from the forced ventilation in the corridor outside allowed him a deep gulp through which he coughed and then shouted his shipmates' names. Taff Evans and Kenny Pullen followed him out in the chaos of the corridor. There were men in various stages of undress and choked shouts of panic rent the acrid gas-filled air.

Tognola looked back through the smoke and saw flames as big as men leap from Curly Smith's cabin. The cabin between his and Curly's was vacant – and locked. That was the one where the beer crate fire had happened earlier.

Paddy knew Scottish deckhand Jimmy Hamilton was in the cabin next to that with his shipmate. He managed to bang on the door. 'Jimmy, get up, get out. We're on fire!' Paddy didn't get to see if Jimmy got out.

Another mass of smoke blew at him and drove him back. In the panic, he could hear screaming. He fumbled and opened the engine casing door near him, leaving it open behind him as he and Evans got to the engine room's steel ladder that led to the upper deck.

Young Kenny Pullen had disappeared.

Further along the corridor, chief Hughie Williams tried to get from the engine room to investigate and help. He was driven back. The smoke was thicker. Flames were everywhere. Amid it all Hughie saw a figure. It looked like one of the young deckies.

'Help me. Mister Williams, help!' The voice was that of a kid.

'Just a bit further, son. Towards me voice, lad. Towards me voice.'

The kid disappeared and a few seconds later Hughie thought he saw the lad again.

'A bit further, and turn right.'

The boy disappeared again. In panic, he had turned left. A blast of more smoke and flame was seconds behind. Williams had no option but to get out and up on deck. He fled through the engine room. Tognola and Evans were there to help him up the ladder that led to the upper deck.

Williams was shaking.

'There's a kid there. He must be dead. Just a kid. I don't even know his name. He took the wrong turn. I told him right. He turned left. He never came back out.'[2]

Paddy and Taff grabbed Williams up. 'C'mon, chief. You'd better get up and help the boss,' said Paddy.

Chief Williams made for the wheelhouse, and Tognola and Evans were just about to join him when they spotted someone else amid the engine room's smoke and flame.

Paddy shouted down, 'Get to the ladder, mate. I'll help you up.' His eyes grew a bit more used to the smoke. He could see there were two men – one carrying the other over his shoulders, in the way a hunter carries a dead deer. Tognola was still finding it hard to breathe.

'Put him down, pal. You'll not get up wi' both of you.'

'I can't. He's me mate.'

Tognola recognised the voice and in the smoke finally made out the tall, slim figure of Eric Petrini.

'Eric, mate, you're gonna have to lay him down!'

'I can't. It's Chuck. Chuck O'Dell.'

'Eric, we'll come back for him. I promise. You'll both be dead otherwise. C'mon Eric. Leave him. You're gonna have to…'

Eric laid down his friend.

'I'll get back for you, Chuck. I'll get back.'

Chuck O'Dell was laid in the alleyway outside the engine room. His body was still. Petrini stumbled, retching and coughing through the smoke to escape. When Petrini had reached the top, more flames engulfed the corridor. At the top of the ladder Tognola helped Petrini. Eric was in a checked shirt and trousers. The shirt was ripped open, revealing burns to his neck and chest. His face was blackened, barring trickle lines put there by sweat… and tears.

There was no going back.

Engineer George Grinlaw had been on watch for little more than five minutes and made his way to the engine room after breakfast. He saw smoke rage through it and pour out the door from which the others had escaped a minute or so earlier. He looked to the door and decided to see if he could see where the flames and smoke had come from. The room was overwhelmed by it. He tried to phone the bridge to raise the alarm. It did not work. He struggled towards the upper deck and the bridge.

Dave Whittaker appeared at the wheelhouse. Sawyer and Bosun Samms were there. Whittaker shouted, 'Fire! All the men's cabins are on fire, boss!'

Sawyer immediately ran past Whittaker, determined to find out what had happened and what he could do. Samms followed. They reckoned there were as many as twenty men down there. They tried to go down to the corridor but made it only a matter of feet before a mass of smoke and flame drove them back. They had no breathing apparatus. They all got back to the bridge. Taff Evans arrived. Tognola was now on deck with Petrini.

Sawyer shouted, 'Taff, get the alarms set off!' The skipper then grabbed the knife from the sheath on the Welshman's belt. 'Gimme it here, Taff!' Sawyer snapped as he took the knife.

He used its handle to smash the glass to set off the emergency alarms. Klaxons sounded. In the wheelhouse Collier pulled on his sea boots. Second engineer Trevor Hardwick struggled in carrying sets of breathing apparatus he had grabbed from an upper deck cupboard. He had been on watch since 0130hours. Grinlaw was his replacement. Hardwick's appearance startled Evans.

'Where the hell did you come from, Trev?'

'I was blown up here, Taff! I tried to get to the engine room. Davy told me about the fire when I was in the mess having summat to eat. I couldn't get back. I put a wet scarf around my face. It was dry in seconds. The smoke's everywhere. Then there was like a big gust. It blew me backwards. There's no getting back.'

Chief Williams said, 'He's right. Let's get the hell out of here.'[3]

Sawyer replied, 'Right, Hughie. Get the men and get to the lifeboats. Try and get the hose working if you can.'

'This one is beyond hoses, boss,' Williams said to Sawyer as he and the men left for the decks. Sawyer shouted, 'Hughie, get all the accessible fuel tanks shut off. Now!' Sawyer stopped the main engines and left the generator and service pumps running, so the men could use the hoses. The hose storage cupboard was red hot. It could not be opened. Even if it could, it was certain its contents were rendered useless. When they finally forced it open they saw there were holes burned in them. Williams and his men shut off the switches for the oil tanks on the boat deck using the controls on the upper deck.

There were two life rafts each stored port and starboard – and the big crew-sized lifeboat was on the davit.

Two deckhands were blown backwards at the same time as they tried to release the lifeboat.

'It's fucking live, boss,' one of the fallen men shouted to Williams. Sawyer was now beside them and tried to release the lifeboat gripe. He too was thrown backwards by the electric shock.

At the port side, another deckie at the life raft store shouted, 'Them bastards are burned up. We're fucked.' The ship shook, lurched in the waves, rose and dropped. The men were thrown into each other. Williams, Samms and a few others managed to grab the starboard-side life rafts.

These were undamaged. Someone shouted, 'Get starboard rafts aft! Put one o'er each side!' Sawyer tried to get into the wireless room. The moment he opened its door, a mass of smoke pushed him back. He returned to the wheelhouse. There was no sign of Tommy Gray. Sawyer shut the door, sprinted back, grabbed the VHF and frantically started turning tuners and flicking switches.

'Mayday! Mayday! This is the Hull trawler *St Finbarr*, Hull trawler *St Finbarr*! Fire on board. Fire on board! Over.'

He heard a familiar voice reply, 'Tommy, it's Eddie Wooldridge. Last I checked I was about five miles from you, I think. What's your exact position… Over…?'

'Eddie, I can't give you a position. Over… The ship is on fire everywhere… full of smoke… Over… I will put all the lights on that I can. I am going around in circles… Over.'[4] Sawyer flicked at every switch he could. Simultaneously, he manually turned his ship head into wind. (The automatic equipment was still dead.) He tried to repeat the Mayday, in case anyone was nearer than Wooldridge's ship, the *Orsino*.

As the ship turned and raised there was a gigantic rumble like rolling thunder. Sawyer grabbed the VHF telephone receiver with one hand, holding the steering gear with the other.

'Mayday!..........'

He was blinded.

He rose at speed from the floor and was thrown through the air like a ragdoll. He was unconscious when he went through the wheelhouse window pane. Flames followed him out.[5] Every wheelhouse window pane blew out simultaneously.

Outside on the aft deck, a series of explosions drowned out the shouting. All the men looked towards the rear of the wheelhouse and saw its doors fly off. They were deafened by the bang that followed. Instinctively they ducked and threw themselves down as the doors clattered past overhead, followed by clouds of smoke of up to twenty feet. The fire took hold. The men could feel intense heat under their feet. Fire spread from the wheelhouse to the bow. The ship rails were hot. Sawyer was laid out cold on a funnel under the wheelhouse front. A gnarled, melted telephone receiver with a singed, snapped cord hanging from it was in his right hand. Twists of smoke rose from the cord. His body was positioned as if it was inside a chalk outline in a cop drama.

Seconds earlier the fireball had blinded him. He had crashed on to the ledge casing. Sawyer was dead still. The wheelhouse front plates (wall) were a sheet of fire. Burning paint was blistering and fiery gobbets of it rained down. Fumes filled Sawyer's lungs with acrid smoke. His sweater and moleskin trousers were blackened and scorched. He had only one suede shoe on.

He started to come to. His ears were still ringing. He looked up. Flames leapt from the eighteen windows of the wheelhouse. Its whole exterior was ablaze and flames were inches from him. The still-dazed skipper instinctively jumped from the casing to the deck below. There he picked up his other shoe and put it back on. He saw flames and smoke belching from the accommodation corridor under his wheelhouse and could feel the soles of his feet burning. The deck was hot – and getting hotter.

At that moment, for all he knew, he was the only man left alive. He struggled to compose himself. Ringing from his ears subsided enough for him to be aware of screams and shouts that told him he was not alone.

The previous few minutes played back in his head. He remembered shouting a Mayday and the voice of his friend Eddie Wooldridge, skipper of the *Orsino*, replying. The horror of what had just happened rapidly came back to him. Help was on the way. That much he knew. Seven minutes earlier he was looking forward to coming off duty and putting a ship-to-shore call for his kids as a Christmas surprise. Now he was not sure he would ever see them again.

On the *Orsino*, Skipper Wooldridge was in the wireless room. The Christmas radio traffic was burbling away as international messages flew through the airwaves. Sparks Bill Dunn was at the radio sets. Wooldridge told him, '*Finbarr*'s on fire, Bill. The electrics are gone. Their radio's gone too. Tommy Sawyer doesn't even have a map reference for us.'

Dunn replied, 'Right skipper,' and immediately set about putting out a further Mayday on the *St Finbarr*'s behalf. His first message read, 'ATTENTION ALL SHIPPING... PROCEEDING ST FINBARR... BRIDGE ON FIRE.' Dunn then changed frequencies and sent another message, 'ATTENTION ALL SHIPPING... ST FINBARR ON FIRE... ALL SHIPPING PLEASE PROCEED TO THE AREA.'[6] The Babel-babble of international Christmas radio traffic halted in seconds. All the telegrams and yuletide ship-to-shore calls immediately stopped and gave way to the emergency. Shipping across the Grand Banks and beyond responded to the Mayday and passed it on.

Among them were the English trawlers, *Sir Frederick Parkes* and *Ross Illustrious*. Along with the *Orsino* these and several other ships set courses towards the *St Finbarr* as quickly as the treacherous sea would allow.

On the *St Finbarr*, the men were gathered aft. The blaze took hold. Smoke now enveloped the wheelhouse and rose to touch cold, dark, steely clouds. The men had managed to get a life raft with them. This was a remarkable feat given the life raft storage units were ablaze. Some men were half-naked, the others in indoor clothes. None were clothed for the outside.

Sawyer appeared from the smoke and staggered aft. The look on their faces told him that they had thought him dead from the wheelhouse blast. He had with him a second life raft. He had braved the flames to stagger with it aft. The skipper quickly counted the group. Fourteen. Some were jumping up and down, others, those without proper foot-wear, moved from one part of the white-hot deck to another to find cooler parts on which they could stand. The deck was freezing and burning up at the same time in differing parts. The deck got hotter and the winds colder. Sawyer led the men from the aft deck into the relative shelter of the net loft and addressed the remainder of his panic-stricken crew. They were already beginning to fade.

'There's help on the way. We have all got to stay calm. We've got to work to get the life rafts over. Most of all we need to stay calm and get the rafts over the side.'

A minute later, Paddy Tognola set off. Before anyone could stop him, he sprinted towards the drying room, which was belching smoke.

'Where the hell are you going, Paddy?' Sawyer shouted.

'Back in a minute. There's clothes in there. These guys are freezing to death.'

He disappeared towards the accommodation deck from which they had just escaped minutes earlier and headed for the drying room, where he knew there were lots of overalls.

Paddy got back almost as quickly as he had gone. He managed to grab piles of overalls which were eagerly grabbed from him by those that needed them most.

Skipper Sawyer was back in control and joined by chief Williams and first mate Walter Collier. The captain's mental roll call listed the men on deck: Tognola, Petrini, Evans, Samms, Hardwick, Gray, Curly Smith, Whittaker, Prince, Grinlaw, Bull and Scott. Fifteen men in all, with himself and the two senior officers included. All of them had little or no sleep in the past twenty-four hours. They were in various stages of exhaustion, but driven by the determination and the primal desire to survive.

Numbness, prickly skin and muscle stiffness was felt by the men to varying degrees. This meant frostbite was kicking in. Soon those men were out on the aft again. The two remaining useable life rafts were cast slowly over the sides by two separate small teams. On the starboard side two deckhands clambered down into the life raft that hung over the side. Once inside the tent-like inflatable, the two men felt it suddenly slip. Both got out and clambered as quickly as they could toward the rail, where their comrades pulled them back on deck. The life raft seemed to slip. The ship rose and fell on a huge wave. The men on the starboard side let out a collective, heart-rending loud groan, like a yell of pain.

'Fuck, it's gone. It's gone!'

This angry, tearful deckhand's shout followed the collective primal scream as the life raft drifted from its lines. A violent rise and fall of the ship shook the life raft lines free from its fixings. It simply had not been secured properly and was washed away.

Clumsiness is an early symptom of frostbite.[7] Lashing ropes and fixing wires is a difficult job in clement conditions, but for these men, in winds of up to forty-five miles an hour and waves of more than thirty feet, it was beyond them. The life raft drifted off, bobbing violently. It quickly became a faraway dot. The broken men rushed to the port side of the aft deck to join their shipmates to ensure the same fate would not befall their last hope. Almost two hours had passed. Death drew nearer to them all again.

A stern trawler was spotted, no more than a mile away. From it a light shone, cutting through the dark winter sea. It illuminated the aft of *St Finbarr*. Along the deck rail of the far-off trawler was a group of men. Some had hands cupped around their mouths, like makeshift megaphones. Their cries perished on the wind as the ship drew nearer to the desperate men of *St Finbarr*. The searchlight's beam dragged from aft to hull and back.

Rescue could not come quickly enough.

CHAPTER EIGHT

From the *Orsino's* bridge skipper Eddie Wooldridge saw *St Finbarr's* wheelhouse and fore deck enveloped in fire and smoke. The aft deck was clear and there were about a dozen or so men milling about, some barely dressed.

'They must be freezing to death there,' the skipper thought as he looked through his binoculars and saw those men as they apparently tried to lower life rafts either side. Flames shot up from the bridge of the stricken ship into the gunmetal grey, dark Labrador skies.

At the *Orsino's* deck rails, bosun George Patrick fixed a searchlight beam on to the burning trawler. The beam moved steadily from aft to hull and back repeatedly. Wooldridge was both stunned and relieved when the familiar figure of skipper Sawyer came briefly into view. The abrupt end of their earlier VHF exchange made the *Orsino's* commander fear the worst. Radio communication was impossible. He tried to count the men. That was nigh-on impossible too. Ten? Twelve? More? One thing was certain; the crew was at least halved.

'Poor bastards,' he thought.

He saw life rafts either side of the aft deck and then spotted two men clamber down to the starboard life raft. The skipper decided to get as close as he could. He assumed Sawyer had given the order to abandon ship. In what seemed like seconds, Wooldridge saw the same two men clamber back aboard. The *St Finbarr* disappeared temporarily into the trough of a giant wave. It reappeared in time for him to see the starboard life raft washed away.

The front of the *St Finbarr* was still buried in flame and smoke. What Wooldridge saw was deceptive. The clouds seemed bigger because steam added to the volume and density. Each time a huge icy, slushy wave hit the white-hot hull it instantly evaporated – when usually it would have iced up. The ship was assailed by ice, fire and water simultaneously. The *Orsino's* radio operator Bill Dunn's emergency messages had been successful and a handful of vessels were soon within a mile of the *St Finbarr*. The *Orsino* was closest. The *Sir Frederick Parkes* and the *Ross Illustrious*, two new modern Hull stern trawlers, were also near.

It was clear that the under-dressed, exhausted survivors on the aft deck were perishing fast. Wooldridge knew they were frostbitten and that it would not be long before these men began to die.

Getting two ships close enough to effect a rescue is a dangerous task. Trawlers rarely came within a mile of each other, even in calm waters, especially when fishing, as catching up in another ship's trawl endangered both. That day Wooldridge's problem was that the churning, mountainous seas and high winds could throw together two ships of more than 1,000 tons each into collision and send both to the bottom.

He needed to get near enough to get the life raft and for the stricken survivors to get aboard but stay a safe distance from the burning trawler. This was Eddie Wooldridge's biggest test of seamanship, and two ships, two crews and two holds full of fish depended on him getting it right.

Setting up a breeches buoy rig with bosun chair was both impossible and ineffective. That sort of setup was for calm waters. Plus, even if it was possible, it would take too long.

The freezing weather and the massive swell made it both impracticable and dangerous. The best way was to get the men into a raft and get that raft towards the *Orsino*. Bosun Patrick had put a rope and wood ladder over the side, behind which was a mass of scramble netting to give something more to grab should a man's grip slip.

Minutes earlier, *Orsino* wireless man Bill Dunn told Wooldridge that another nearby Hull trawler the *Sir Frederick Parkes* had tried unsuccessfully to fire a line on to the *St Finbarr* to try to get some clothing and supplies on to the ship. Not only did the raging sea beat them but also the extremely fatigued handful of men were unable to successfully pull the line in.

Dunn had been in conversation with several ships' radio men. About ten ships, British and foreign, were now in the area. More were on the way. Wooldridge told Dunn to ask them all to stand by but added that the rescue would be carried out by him and his crew. The men aft of the *St Finbarr* watched as the *Orsino* hove close in. They were dwarfed by the rescue vessel as she rose on a massive wave and passed the stricken ship's stern. The *Orsino* pulled alongside and rose astern again like a sea monster thrusting from a B-movie ocean and the waves that followed her drop swept over the freezing trawlermen.

On her rails, *Orsino's* bosun and a group of deckhands shouted and gestured, flailing and screeching to try to get the message across.

'Get them into the raft, let them drift, we'll get them!' shouted Patrick. The others repeated the message both vocally and in desperate mime. It must have gotten through. From the *Orsino's* bridge, Wooldridge saw some men head to a life raft that was draped over the side.

Three miles away, Bob Laing, wireless operator of Hull trawler *Ross Illustrious*, also took the Mayday from *St Finbarr*. He rushed to the wheelhouse. Skipper Roy Waller was at the bridge.

'*St Finbarr*'s on fire, skipper. We've been asked to go to her.' Other men might have blurted this out, but Laing, a cool, dapper, pencil-moustached Scot, with a reputation for being a cool head in a crisis, was not such a man.

'Get back to them, Bob,' Waller said, 'Let them know we're on our way. What's their position?'

'Haven't got one. It's a bad fire. Tommy Sawyer is taking her in circles with as many lights as possible. *Orsino* is nearest and we'll get details from them.'

'In this weather, we'll be lucky to make five knots. OK, Bob. Get back to the wireless set and tell them we'll be there in the hour.'

With that, Waller took the Tannoy microphone, from near his VHF radio set. He knew his first mate Lawrie Wildman was on the factory deck waiting for the haul. Waller sounded the klaxon and made his announcement. 'Attention all crew.

Stow the trawl. Close the doors. Repeat, stow the trawl, close the doors. This is an emergency.'

Aft on the trawl deck the men set about pulling in the massive nets so they could get the stern fishing deck doors closed as quickly as possible.

Below decks, mate Wildman with the factory deck men dealt with the haul to be processed. Wildman strained to hear the message and turned to teenage deckhand Ray Hawker.

'Ray, kid, run up to the bridge and see what that bastard wants. I can't hear a fucking thing. That Tannoy has been fucked for weeks. Just go and see what he wants.'

The nineteen-year-old deckhand was on the upper deck in a minute and at his skipper's side less than half that time again.

The breathless young man blurted, 'Mate's sent me, skipper. He can't hear the Tannoy. Wants to know what you want.'

'What I want, kid, is the trawl stowed, the doors up and the catch dealt with pronto. There's an incident we got to get to. Tell him to get a move on.'

Young Ray turned and ran back to the factory deck and relayed the message. Within minutes Wildman took two hands with him and helped stow the trawl with the other on the stern and got the stern-deck door closed in double time. He then rejoined the factory deck men to help process the catch. Waller's estimate was spot on. Well within the hour his ship was near the rescue ship *Orsino*. Bob Laing told Bill Dunn they would stay on standby as long as they were needed. From his bridge Waller peered through binoculars and saw the blazing trawler, the rescue ship and several other vessels scattered around the heaving waters.

Even in the dark overcast morning he recognised the silhouettes of another four Hull ships. He strained to count how many men he could see aft of the *St Finbarr*. This was made more difficult by the cloud drifts of smoke from the blazing wheelhouse. Waller's cursory glances of the ship's plates told him the Hull super-trawler was in more trouble. Some of those plates were coming apart. This told him that the intense heat had expanded the metal and it would not be long until water found its way through. Waller hoped the *Orsino* would get about her rescue fast.

The *Ross Illustrious*, owned by British United Trawlers (BUT) of Hull, was on its second trip and had been launched only a few months earlier. She was launched as a joint venture between the Ross Food Group and Hellyer Brothers of Hull, under the BUT banner. She was one of a handful of recent stern trawlers launched to try to copy the success of the record-breaking *St Finbarr*. *Ross Illustrious'* skipper Roy Waller was a very able man who also had the unusual accolade of being one of the few commanders both respected and liked by his crewmen. He had arranged for the crew to have Christmas dinners in rota at the below-decks mess. By the time she had come near the *Orsino,* the men of the *Ross Illustrious* factory deck had processed the catch and headed to the mess room for their food.

An incongruity of Christmas tunes crackled through the radio and provided borderline-surreal background music for the forlorn men gathered either side of the long table covered with food and drinks. Those seated could see the stricken ship, and a dozen or so desperate men shivering on the aft deck, through the portholes either side of the mess room. There was no appetite but men ate, driven by hunger resulting from eighteen-hour shifts that burned 6,000 or 7,000 calories. Heavy hearts and souls did not suppress empty stomachs. It would not have mattered if it was turnip or turkey, they had to eat. Just 500 yards from their table, men lay dead, killed instantly below decks of a blazing ship to the aft of which a further dozen or so were freezing to death. There was no relishing food or marking the day, but for the grace of God went they.

At one porthole, an older deckhand fixedly stared out. Ted Coulman, one of Waller's best men and a mentor to younger deckhands, could not come away from the rain-lashed glass.

'My brother's lad is on that ship,' Ted said. 'I just can't see if he's there or not.'

At the Christmas table five minutes later, they forced their food down as the old deckhand walked past in silence and headed for the upper deck, not knowing that his brother's son was dead.[1] When the old deckhand left, the sombre silence in his wake was broken by a shipmate: 'Can somebody turn that stupid fucking radio off.'

Back on the *St Finbarr* skipper Sawyer ordered his crew to abandon ship. The men boarded the remaining safe life raft.

'Get in, lads. Eddie Wooldridge's lads will pick you up. Won't be long now.'

The exhausted, frozen, part-frostbitten men lumbered to the raft. Ropes creaked as it filled.

Sawyer said, 'I'm staying with her. I have to stay while there's still a chance of saving her.'

Everyone knows that the captain staying with his ship is a tradition of the sea, but if you were the man that had to do it, it was clearly the ultimate test of bravery. This was not only extraordinary courage by Sawyer but it also made commercial sense in his eyes. The ship and the men were insured. The catch was not. He knew there was every chance his burning ship could be towed in before the frozen block deep in the hold would be rendered rotten by defrosting. Sawyer's two senior officers had obviously been thinking along the same lines. So, the accepted protocol of the skipper, mate and engineer staying to save the vessel was agreed among the three. Mate Collier said, 'I'm wi' you, boss.'

'Me too,' chief Williams added, 'I know every bit of this ship. We still have a chance of getting her in and landing the catch.'

The three ship's officers helped the raft full of men stutter its way down the side of the ship. A big swell lapped at the little craft as it neared the ogin. Ropes were not well fixed and as it hit the sea its weight almost forced it under. A mass of water gushed through the flaps. It took a few seconds for the raft to settle. Those seconds seemed like hours and the twelve weakened survivors gripped as tightly as they could as the little boat righted. It floated and drifted toward the massive *Orsino*.

Icy sea water came up past the thighs of the already-numbed men in the raft. There was a baling pump, but no-one was strong enough to use it – even if they were, the collective clumsiness of their early-onset frostbite made it futile. They sat silently in the raft, lit dimly by a wire-covered lamp. They quietly hoped for the ordeal to end soon – but most of all hoped that their tiny craft would stay above the waves until their rescue.

Back on the *St Finbarr*, Sawyer, Collier and Williams retreated to the net loft for the little shelter it offered in that frozen hell.

Attached to every life raft, dinghy or lifeboat is a painter's rope, sometimes known as a painter's line, so called because it allowed painters to get close to ships that they needed to work on using such craft. It was there to be tied up or pulled on to drag a boat in. In the case of the *St Finbarr* life raft, the plaited nylon rope attached was about an inch in circumference and maybe three fathoms (eighteen feet) long. It was bright white, and dashes of high-visibility orange tape alternated along its length. It floated and drifted out alongside, as it was designed to do. It resembled a very long, thin sidewinder snake as it moved randomly on the surface. The *Orsino*'s bosun saw it rise and fall in the swell. He had a difficult manoeuvre to make. He needed to snag the painter's rope and somehow get it on board so it could be used to drag the life raft close to the wood and rope ladder and scramble net hung over the side. The ladder and netting dipped in and out of the waves as the Orsino rose and dropped. The bosun could have fired a line into the raft for the men to tie up, but the earlier experience with the *Sir Frederick Parkes'* effort to get supplies to the *St Finbarr* told him this would not work. The men were too weak.

There are a few ways to fire a line. If the target is near enough it is simply a matter of throwing a heaving line towards it for the men to pick it up. At the end of that heaving line is a knot known as a "monkey's fist" – a large end-knot of rope lashed from a length. This enables a larger line that could not be thrown over the distance to be pulled over. The most common use of a heaving line at sea is to pull a cable to shore from a ship.

Sometimes the monkey's fist knot can have a small weight, a stone or ball-bearing at its core, to make it go further. Another option open to the bosun was to use the Schermully gun, like the one famously brandished by Hull skipper Phil Gay.

The Schermully looked like an old brass flintlock pistol into the long, wide barrel of which a line, or indeed a flare, could be placed to be fired. The line fired could have the monkey's fist attachment picked up by the men targeted.[2] The thin line fired was usually attached to a bigger one that would be pulled in. This was out of the question for the bosun too. The only real option was to snag the painter's rope. The plan was to fire a line with a grappling hook where the monkey's fist would have been. The hooked line would be dragged into the painter's rope and would hopefully be twisted sufficiently to allow the bosun's men to drag it in. He had to be careful not to overshoot it. A grappling hook hitting the raft would not be good news.

On a good calm sea, this rescue would have been so much easier. A breeches buoy and a bosun's chair could have been set up between the stricken ship and the rescue vessel. That day, in those raging seas, this was not possible.

The men were off the blazing ship. So far everything seemed to have conspired against them: the weather, losing a raft, being unable to launch the big lifeboat. They could not catch a break.

Inside the raft, the first man to board, greaser John Scott, must have been one of the most confused souls there. Earlier he had been having a post-breakfast smoke on the aft at the end of his watch when the entire ship seemed to explode. Now, from the opening in the life raft, all he could see was swelling waves and occasionally the *Orsino* as she hove into view when one of those waves lifted the tiny craft carrying the twelve exhausted, bewildered men. It was being thrown about like a cork in a swirling tub. Soon the men felt the craft being pulled.

The *Orsino* bosun's Schermully gun, or rather the deckhand who aimed it, had done the job. A grappling hook snagged the painter's line and it was pulled towards the *Orsino*. Relief was not expressed in the raft; the survivors were stunned quiet, scared and frostbitten.

For forty-five minutes, they sat in that life raft before it was eventually pulled in and tied to the *Orsino*. The open flap of the raft faced the dangling rope ladder, behind which was the large scrambling net.

Holding on to a rope ladder, let alone climbing one, in high seas is a daunting task for a fit and able man. For this dozen bedraggled, frostbitten wretches it was a potential death sentence. The younger, stronger men's stamina and chances of successfully completing the climb were higher, but only marginally. The rope ladder with its wooden rungs dangled and swayed in the high winds despite the deckhands' best efforts to steady it. It was about a twenty-five-feet climb, the equivalent of scaling the side of a terraced house's gable end.

The silence in the raft was palpable as each man concentrated on the terrifying task ahead. First to reach out from the raft to the ladder was radio man Tommy Gray. The fifty-year-old was brave and strong but frostbite had taken effect. His numbed hands, prickling with pins and needles, grabbed the ropes either side. Using all his upper body strength he managed to get on to the rungs. He pulled himself free of the raft and fully on to the ladder.

Above him a further twenty feet or so of ladder swung in the wind. Gray had to get up as fast as he could. The swell meant the ship rose and fell and dipped him in the raging waters. The ship's rising and falling could easily throw him. He gripped as tightly as he could and moved on to the second rung.

The *Orsino* rose on a wave, then fell, and she took Gray and the ladder into the confused sea. When the bottom of the ladder was visible again it was clear Gray had been thrown from it. He had only managed to get on to the second rung before being cast backwards into the swirling waters. He fought furiously to try to swim back. The final words heard in his life were from desperate men on the *Orsino*'s rails.

'C'mon, c'mon... you can do it... c'mon swim, swim...' The men cheered him on like they would a winger going for a try at the Boulevard. They were willing him to get back.

The shouting stopped when Tommy Gray disappeared.

The *Orsino* men had no time to do anything other than to get the next man on the ladder.

In the raft Paddy Tognola saw the radio operator fall. The young deckhand still found it difficult to breathe; his smoke-damaged lungs fought for each gulp of air. He was not sure if the others had seen Tommy Gray fall. There was no talking. And there was no gasp or other noise when the radio man fell. Tognola tried to put everything to the back of his mind and concentrated solely on how he would tackle that ladder when his turn came.

The young deckhand's feet had gone from prickly to completely numb.

When Harry Prince's turn came, he hoped his lifelong luck would hold. He must have thought of the night ten years earlier when his life was saved in a raft like the one he was in now. But back then he was ten years younger, three stones lighter and a lot stronger.

The burly cook steeled himself ready to reach out and grabbed the twisting, jolting ladder that was his only way to safety. He pulled himself upwards by sheer force of will. Step after deliberate step was taken as the swell did its worst and threw the ship.

Harry looked straight up. The supporting shouts of the men on the rail were background noise. He concentrated on every move he made. Each rung took him nearer to safety. Each grip and pull tested his luck. Sheer willpower carried him up the flimsy rope ladder. Then the background noise of the cheering men became audible. Clearer.

The roar of waves lessened. Then Harry felt strong pairs of hands grabbing at his broad shoulders, under his arms, at his clothing, pulling him over the rail.

Harry's luck had held out once more. He fell, exhausted, on to the *Orsino*'s deck.

There was no bravado or quips when determined old greaser Curly Smith steeled himself for his life or death task. He could stand, with a frozen hand on either flap of the raft that steadied him as he prepared to make the most accurate, well-timed and most important jump of his fifty-odd years. The wiry, lithe greaser was a powerfully built little tough guy and timed it perfectly. His bony, strong hands gripped the ropes. His feet flailed until they found a rung to dig into. The ship rose and fell as he climbed. Each move of his hands to the next rung was deliberate and slow. His leg muscles ached from the frostbite and pain seared through the blackened feet under his boots. Each move was a new agony. Every wave threatened to throw him. Above him was the encouragement of the men led by bosun Patrick. Patrick was an old friend of Curly's going back years. But the old greaser could have had little or no idea that the man leading the shouts of encouragement was his mate George. He was fighting for each step and being doused in the water as he started up. He was also drenched by the waves.

Four or five rungs up, Curly's confidence grew. He was getting nearer to the deck and more importantly further from the waves. Curly – in common with many men of the sea – could not swim. Seconds after he made his next step, Curly was under water, but he still clung to the ladder. The *Orsino* dipped and took him with it. The ship rose, and Curly had disappeared.

Bosun Patrick started to climb over the rail. A deckhand grabbed him and shouted, 'What the hell are you doing, boss?'

'I am going to get him. Curly's an old mate. I can't just do nowt.'

'George, if you go down there, you'll be dead in minutes. It'll be you in the water.'

The row between the bosun and deckhand stopped as the ship rose again. Curly was still on the ladder and clung like a limpet. He had managed to keep hold of the scramble net and somehow found himself still on the way up. Icy waters chilled him. He was drenched. He doggedly continued to climb.

'C'mon, Curly,' shouted Patrick, and soon the men at the rails were urging his every step too. Like a slow spider he took rung after rung nearer the rail.

Each step seemed to be followed by a wave or a dip. The trawlerman was frozen, soaked and scared as he got within reach of the *Orsino* men. Then Curly simply vanished. It took just seconds before the men saw him in the water. Whether the wind had blown him from the ladder or he had simply fallen exhausted can never be known, but he plummeted into the swell. From the deck, the *Orsino*'s third engineer Dusty Miller saw his *St Finbarr* counterpart resurface briefly and disappear as quickly again. The men at the rail shouted in vain. Curly was gone.

Eric Petrini, the badly burned deckhand, who earlier was forced to leave his pal "Chuck" O'Dell in the alleyway of the *St Finbarr* accommodation corridor, had one of the hardest fights to get aboard the *Orsino*. Each survivor thus far had managed the climb at about five to six minutes per man. This was not only proof, if it were needed, of the toughness of the Hull trawlerman, but was also more remarkable still, since all the men were in varying stages of frostbite and exhaustion. Some had not eaten for hours.

When it came to Eric's turn, the slim, powerfully built young fisherman steeled himself for the climb. He leapt from the raft's mouth and grabbed the ladder. Pain seared through his frostbitten hands and feet with each rung. He let out loud cries. Each contact between rung and hand or foot shot agony through him.

The young deckhand persevered, determined step by step, grip by grip. Salt from the waves weaved its way into the fibre of his skin via the burns on his neck, chest and shoulders. The men left in the life raft watched as he got nearer to the rail, inspired and awed by his gritty progress. It took him twice as long as those who had gone before – but he made it.

Even the toughened men of the *Orsino*, who had seen more that day than most would in a lifetime, winced as they dragged Petrini over the rail and saw the mottled reds and purples of his burned skin and the frostbitten blackened tips of his feet and hands. Deckhands grabbed at his torn shirt and gripped his arms and upper body to heave him over.

He fell to the deck and yelped in pain, but was soon on his feet and sat with the others so far saved. Those who went before and after Eric were also in varying stages of frostbite. Not one would have lasted another hour. The *Orsino*'s crew helped ten men in total on to their ship alive. Now they had to get the remaining three officers from the burning trawler – and then somehow get the *St Finbarr* towed to shore. *St Finbarr* was at the mercy of sea, ice and fire.

There were flames below her decks and high winds across her bows. Skipper Wooldridge watched his counterpart and his two officers through his binoculars. Earlier he had seen them feebly attempting star jumps to battle the cold before they disappeared. It was obvious to Wooldridge that these men needed to be brought aboard – and soon. While the men at the rails brought the crippled men of *St Finbarr* on deck, the skipper called first mate Bryan Lee to the bridge. 'Take a work boat crew over to Tommy and his men. Get them back here. They ain't going to last much longer on that ship, mate. Get a towline fixed. I will get Bill to radio ahead.'

'The weather will be lighter soon, skipper. We'll get across then. The swell's dropping too.'

'Don't leave it too long, Bryan. Those guys are on their last legs.'

The work boat was launched. An overcast, leaden-skied daylight had come. Wooldridge watched from the bridge as his rescue party headed to the *St Finbarr*. The swell had lessened.

Wooldridge peered through the binoculars and saw his men progress towards the blighted ship. Sawyer's earlier tactic of taking the ship in circles had worked and there was less smoke and flame than previously. Wooldridge could see that mate Lee and the men were making good headway.

CHAPTER NINE

Christmas Day, 1030hours, off the Newfoundland coast.

The *St Finbarr* was a fiery *Mary Celeste*.

The aft deck, from the where the raft full of men was launched by Sawyer and his two officers, was now empty. Parallel to the stricken trawler the *Orsino* waited. Each rose and fell on violent waves. There were still other ships dotted on the waters around. But on the empty aft of the blazing ship an eerie silence pervaded, broken only by the occasional whoosh of waves as they crashed over the decks. The fore still blazed and smoke and steam wrapped the ship in a rising, twisting, amorphous acrid cloud. When the wind rose, the cloud cleared aft and then returned on the falling of the gust.

Sawyer, Collier and Williams could not be seen. *Orsino* first mate Bryan Lee and his four deckhands clambered aboard aft, where the three officers were last sighted by Wooldridge. Lee's portable radio set was not working well in the harsh conditions, but he managed to message back to his captain.

'We'll try the net loft, skipper. It's the only place they can be, if they're still aboard.'

He beckoned two of the rescue party to bring the bags that contained food and clothes they had brought with them from the work boat, which was now tied to the trawler.

The net loft on the fish deck was, like the rest of vessel, in darkness. In among the nets Lee could see three men. Initially, he feared he had arrived too late when the beam of his flashlight criss-crossed the motionless trio. One was dressed in an open-necked shirt, moleskin trousers and shoes, the second was in engineer's brown overalls and boots and the third in fearnought trousers, gansey and boots. Lee's flashlight settled upon their pale, bluing faces.

He turned to his men and shouted, 'Get over here, now.'

Lee leaned over the three trawlermen. He knew them all but hardly recognised them. They were barely alive. The ailing men's clothing was soaked through, icy and clung to them. One of Lee's deckhands unloaded the fresh clothing while the mate talked to the men.

Lee said, 'Don't worry, lads, we'll soon have you out.'

The three moaned replies.

'Gimme them scissors and get them clothes o'er here,' Lee said. He began to cut the clothing from Hughie Williams. Of the three stricken men, the chief engineer looked closest to death. He had only light overalls, sufficient for the boiling heat of the engine room but now not much better than being naked. He was in pain from frostbite in his feet and, like his two fellow officers, was exhausted.

Lee and a couple of his deckhands rubbed vigorously at the men's skin, to get the blood circulating. As they cut through the clothes it was clear that frostbite had advanced in them all. There was blackening of the feet. The men let out occasional yelps of agony as Lee and his crew set about getting them dressed. But the chief engineer still looked the weakest of the three.

Icy winds, driving sleet and punishing waves had earlier forced Sawyer, Collier and Williams from the aft deck to stay in the net loft after the other men had gone. Ironically, there was some warmth from the heat conducted through the ship's plates and deck by the flames to the fore.

The exhausted trio clustered together as close as they could in the hope that what was left of any collective body heat would help them. Brandy taken from mate Lee's haversack was drunk with the relish a greedy child would have for soda pop. The three men sank two large tots each in rapid succession as Lee and his deckhands dressed and treated them. Williams still looked the worst of the trio.

Lee stayed with the three while his men went back on the aft deck.

He spoke to Sawyer, 'Skipper, we're going to put the towline on and try to get her back to St John's. When the lads have got it hitched up we'll have you all out of here.'

Sawyer murmured his approval. Collier sat up, let out a sudden yelp and lay down. His breathing was laboured. He was obviously in pain. He suddenly looked as bad as Williams. Lee could not figure out why. What Collier could not explain was that his stomach ulcer had perforated. The pain rendered him dumb and he began to slip in and out of consciousness.

'C'mon, Walt. Don't give up now,' Lee said. 'We'll be out of here soon enough.'

Outside the men on the aft waited for a line to be shot to them from the *Orsino*. Bosun Patrick and his men fired it from the Schermully gun with ultimate precision and within minutes the *Orsino* rescue party were pulling a tow warp aboard.

This was to be attached to the warp coiled on the winch of the *St Finbarr*. It was the only possible link they could safely attach. The ship would be towed stern first. The fore was still ablaze and the heat-expanded plates had allowed water in. Effectively the bow was dipped down, so to tow that way around would have driven her underwater very quickly. Wooldridge had told his rescue party to concentrate on getting a stern tow fixed.

They were 240 miles from St John's. With a potential top speed of about five knots, the skipper figured it would be forty-eight hours to landing. He knew getting a tow attached would not be a swift business either. It was more than just fixing two lines together and setting off.

Firstly, the men would now have to get the main warp aboard from the *Orsino*. This meant pulling in the line that was fired across, which in turn was attached to the heavier warp from the rescue ship. It was going to take at least an hour to drag the thick steel-rope warp through the raging waves. Even in rubber duck suits, gloves and heavy boots, working on deck for that long in that weather pulling a heavy warp through the water (a job usually done by a motor winch) was a labour-intensive, tiring task, especially with the added problem of the rise and fall of both ships in the swell. Snow blizzarded as the *Orsino*'s men worked. Speed was of the essence if the three men in the net loft were to stand a chance.

Mate Bryan Lee decided to check the ship while his men worked. For now, he had done all he could for the men in the net loft. He took two deckies with him, in case there was anything that could be salvaged.

The trio could feel the heat through the thick soles of their Arctic work boots. The heat increased as they drew nearer the hull. Flames still shot from the windowless wheelhouse.

Lee left his men briefly and ventured to try to go inside the burned-out wheelhouse. He got as far as the part-opened bridge door. It was red hot to the touch.

Where the VHF transmitter had been, Lee saw a mass of bubbled, lumpy plastic and twisted metal, interspersed with broken valves. It was all that was left of the world's most expensive trawler's bridge.

The heat was intense and Lee started to return to the aft deck. There was no way anyone could go below or stay forward for long. Lee noted that the *St Finbarr*'s big lifeboat to the back of the wheelhouse was scorched but otherwise OK.

In the *Orsino*'s mess, ten survivors were in dry clothing. Earlier some had had their clothes cut from them. They were in varying stages of exposure and frostbite. Others, who had only the overalls Tognola had found for them, were worse still. The *Orsino* men had gone to their own cabins and brought boots and clothes, booze, cigs and food. In the mess, grateful for their very lives, the men revived visibly, but kept a subdued silence, broken by the occasional mumbled 'thank you'.

Orsino shipmates marvelled at the speed with which colour returned to their faces. Only a few hours earlier they had been the hue of parchment. Some *Orsino* men later gave up their cabins to the *St Finbarr* lads too.

On the bridge Wooldridge grew concerned at the time taken to fix the tow. It was nearly 1300hours and Lee reported from the *St Finbarr* that chief engineer Williams had taken a turn for the worse and was being sent across in the rescue party's boat.

The *Orsino* mate told his boss that Sawyer and Collier, who were somewhat revived but still very weak, insisted on staying and would come later with the boarding party.

1400hours, on the St Finbarr

The *Orsino* work boat was back. The two men disembarked, fastened the craft and then reported to Lee and Sawyer that Williams was safe aboard the *Orsino* and being clothed, fed and warmed. Lee met the two returned men and went to work with the tow party. In the net loft, Sawyer and Collier remained weak but determined. Lee told his team, 'We're going to have to get a move on, lads. The guys in the net loft don't look too good at all.'

The warp from the *Orsino* was now aboard. The men set about the task of fixing it to the *St Finbarr*'s winch.

After fifteen minutes, Lee returned to the net loft to check in on the two men.

'Tommy, Walt, we're going to have to get you off here now. Some of the lads can take you over in the work boat. We'll carry on wi' the tow line.' This time neither skipper Tommy Sawyer nor first mate Walter Collier argued. The *St Finbarr*'s commander feebly gave his final order: 'Time to abandon, ship, eh, Walt?' Sawyer and the mate had spent a little more than seven hours aboard after he had sent the men to the life raft.

Minutes later, while working on the final securing of the towline, rescue party commander mate Bryan Lee could not believe what he had just heard.

'What d'you mean, gone?'

The deckhand simply pointed out over the rail.

'I don't know, boss. It couldn't have been tied-up right. But it's gone.'

The two men and the remainder of the party looked out to sea. They saw the work boat from which they had boarded. It floated further and further away. It had slipped its mooring while the men worked on the towline on deck and kept the two *St Finbarr* officers alive in the net hold. By the time it was noticed it was hundreds of feet from the ship. They were stranded on the burning ship. Another dose of bad luck on this blighted rescue.

'What do we do now?' one of the men said.

'We've got to radio back and get another boat over,' said another.

'We don't have time for that,' Lee replied. 'Those two men in the loft ain't gonna last much longer.'

The mate pointed to the davit behind the wheelhouse.

'The lifeboat,' he said, 'We'll launch that. I looked at it when I came on. It's scorched but it's workable.'

'Yeah, but when one of the *Finbarr* lads was getting on the raft earlier he said they could not launch it because it was electrified,' one of the deckhands added.

Seconds later, Lee stood in front of the lifeboat davit and announced the first lucky break of the day.

'It's fine. Look! No electricity here,' Lee said, his hand rested on the winch mechanism. 'So, come on, let's get this thing in the water and get off this hell.'

The fire, still blazing below and forward, had finally granted the men a boon. All the ship's electrics were dead and the lifeboat could be launched manually. The towline was fixed.

The men had spent hours working on it, knowing a potential explosion might not be far away. Now that the work boat had gone the chances of getting away with any speed from such an explosion had diminished. It was equally possible that an explosion may never come, but they did not want to hang around to test that theory.

Lee knew it was time for them to get to the *Orsino* as quickly as they could, or at least as far away from the blazing ship as possible. The *Orsino*'s mate's thoughts were shattered. A loud rumbling from below decks became a rapid series of bangs. The *St Finbarr* rocked from side to side and then lifted and dropped on the swell. The decision was made for him. It was as if the gremlins that had plagued this ship had been reading the *Orsino* officer's mind.

Within minutes of the explosions, skipper Sawyer and his mate Walt Collier were carried between pairs of deckhands towards the scorched lifeboat at the end of the aft deck where it was readied for descent.

The short series of explosions halted and the ship steadied. Lee and his men acted swiftly. The *St Finbarr* men were first in the lifeboat, being laid side-by-side across the thwarts.

Although somewhat revived by brandy and warm clothing, it was obvious they were struggling, especially Collier.

Mate Lee said to Collier, 'Walt, you look in a bad way, our kid. Just take it easy, won't be long now.'

'I think it's my ulcer, Bry,' the suffering fisherman replied. 'It's getting worse.' The *St Finbarr* mate's breathing was laboured. Lee looked to the pair lying next to each other and repeated, 'Not long now, lads.'

From the *Orsino*'s bridge her skipper saw the scorched lifeboat stutter its way down the side of the blazing trawler. Eddie Wooldridge breathed a sigh of relief, lay down his binoculars, turned to the radio man and said, 'They're coming over, Bill. Tell the bosun and lads to get ready to help winch them on.'

Soon Wooldridge would begin to tow the *St Finbarr*. They would not get above four knots with the blazing vessel being pulled stern first through a confused sea.

It was going to be a long 240 miles to St John's. The skipper figured his course and strategy in the wheelhouse.

Bosun George Patrick and his men on deck readied the winches to raise the lifeboat.

On *Orsino*'s deck now were some of the walking wounded from the doomed ship. A handful held on to the rails with ill-fitting clothing given by the *Orsino* men and looked out to the white lifeboat scarred with black scorch marks as it bobbed and drew slowly ever nearer.[1]

The Perfect Trawler

The *St Finbarr* takes to the water for the first time at the yard of
Ferguson Brothers (Port Glasgow Ltd.) on October 2, 1964.

HDM

The *St Finbarr* ready for her sea trials, October 1964.

HDM

St Finbarr preparing for her maiden voyage.

HDM

The *St Finbarr* ready for her maiden voyage, November 1964. She sailed straight out on her first voyage and landed a national record catch upon her return to Hull.

HDM

The final leave

Jill, left, with her husband Tony and a pal of his in the Alexandra Hotel on Hessle Road, just days before the voyage.

JHL

Tony and Jill Harrison's final night out was at The Maybury pub in mid-November 1966. Next to Tony, far left, is David Young, the *St Finbarr's* deckie learner. Jill is fourth from the left, in the middle of the row. On the far right of the picture, just visible, is Kenny Pullen, *St Finbarr* deckhand. Robert Coulman was at the bar buying a round of drinks when this was taken.

JHL

Harry "Curly" Smith – Hessle Road character

Harry "Curly" Smith larking about with a makeshift French Horn made from an oil funnel and some piping!

RS

A later photograph of Harry Smith, taken at his daughter's wedding shortly before the final trip. At the wedding, Harry told his family he was so pleased they were all together – "because you never know when one of us will be gone."

RS

The rescue bid

Hull trawler *Sir Fred Parkes* in her failed attempt to get a line onto the
St Finbarr. The rescue was soon taken over by another Hull ship the *Orsino*.

RS

The *St Finbarr* minutes into the disaster fully ablaze. These and other
photos of the stricken ship are thought to have been taken by a family
friend of Harry Smith, who was on the *Sir Fred Parkes*.

RS

The rescue boat from the *Orsino*. Its crew of the mate and four deckhands boarded the blazing trawler to rescue the skipper, mate and chief engineer who stayed aboard after getting twelve men off.

RS

Rescue ship *Orsino* perilously close to the blazing *St Finbarr* shortly after the explosion.

GWL

Orsino alongside *St Finbarr* in brief respite in storm before attempts to save twelve men from a life raft.

GWL

Blazing *St Finbarr* blown sideways as rescue crew from the *Orsino's* work boat try to board her by climbing a net.

GWL

The Men of the *St Finbarr*

Heroic first mate, Walt Collier, who with the skipper Tom Sawyer and chief engineer Hughie Williams stayed aboard the blazing vessel at great risk to his own life.

HDM

St Finbarr bosun Eric "Newfie" Samms, who helped lead his shipmates to safety.

HDM

Chief engineer Hughie Williams, who stayed with two other officers aboard the stricken trawler.

HDM

Sparehand Jeff "Chuck" O'Dell the deckhand that brave shipmate Eric Petrini tried in vain to carry to safety.

HDM

Scottish deckhand Jimmy
Hamilton, who had a dram on
the bridge with skipper Tommy
Sawyer after wishing him a
"merry Christmas".

HDM

Sparehand Stanley Brigham.

HDM

Kenny Pullen, deckhand.

HDM)

Johann "Siggy" Sigurdsson.

HDM

Robert Coulman, the young deckhand

HDM

Harry "Curly" Smith taken from his daughter's wedding just days before his final voyage.

HDM

Radio operator Tommy Gray.

HDM

Jack Smith, the fish-room chargehand who wanted to leave the sea to become a publican.

HDM

Deckhand John Matthews.

HDM

Deckhand Tony Harrison, front left and deckie learner David Young from their last night out in Hull together.

HDM

Aftermath

From left, Captain Tom Sawyer, of the *St Finbarr*, Captain Eddie
Wooldridge, of the *Orsino* with the *St Finbarr's* chief engineer Hughie
Williams and first mate Walter Collier at a press conference before
leaving Newfoundland for home, December 29, 1966.

HDM

Back home. Tom Sawyer, second left wearing trilby hat, with some of
the *St Finbarr* crew coming through customs at Prestwick Airport in
Scotland.

HDM

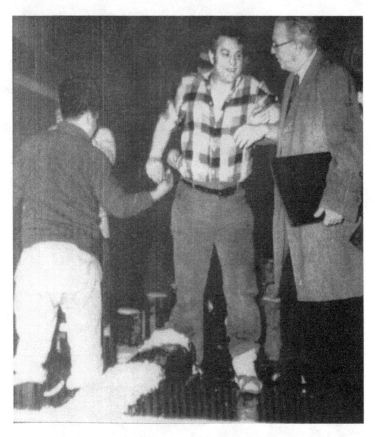

Canadian shipping agent from Bowring's of St John's helps rescued
St Finbarr crewman disembark from the *Orsino*.

HDM

One crewman from the *St Finbarr* helps deckhand Paddy Tognola
disembark from the rescue ship *Orsino* on the same ladder that
48 hours earlier helped save their lives.

HDM

Brave deckhand Eric Petrini, who tried in vain to save his shipmate Jeff "Chuck" O'Dell, avoids one press cameraman at Prestwick Airport, Scotland, only to be caught by a second.

HDM

Hull-born singer and panto star Ronnie Hilton with orphaned children backstage at the Hull New Theatre Christmas 1967. The uniformed men are from the Fishermen's Mission.

HDM

Author's Note

Most of the photographs here are from the archives of the *Hull Daily Mail* – these are marked "HDM"

Photos from Mr Ron Smith (son of Harry "Curly" Smith) are marked "RS"

The family of the late George William Lee provided on-the-spot photographs taken on the Grand Banks that fateful day. They are initialled "GWL"

Photographs, courtesy of Mrs Jill Taylor Harrison Long, widow of sparehand Tony Harrison, are marked "JHL"

PART TWO

THE QUIET DISASTER

Blazing trawler sinks in gale

— **From VICTOR DAVIS:**
St John's, Newfoundland, Tuesday.
(Daily Express, Wednesday, December 28, 1966.)

"In Britain it was the quiet disaster. [...] not until tonight did details of the Christmas morning disaster in the gale-swept Atlantic leak through"

FROM CHRISTMAS DAY RADIO/TELEGRAM TRAFFIC*

FROM LLOYDS TELEX, LONDON AT 1850 25.12.

'ST FINBARR FROM OFFICER IN CHARGE CARTWRIGHT RADIO LABRADOR 1230 GMT, 25/12 FOLLOWING DISTRESS MESSAGES RECEIVED FROM TRAWLER "SIR FRED. PARKES" AS 840AM GMT TODAY 25/12 ST FINBARR QFXU ON FIRE POSITION LATITUDE 55 15 W LONGITUDE 55 4 N TEN MEN RESCUED TWO MEN WERE LOST THIRTEEN UNACCOUNTED FOR AS OF NOON GMT STOP VESSELS "SIR FRED PARKES" AND TRAWLER "ORSINO" STANDING BY AND ATTEMPTING RESCUE OF REMAINING MEN'

TO MASTER, SIR FRED PARKES AT 2015, 25/12

'PLEASE PASS ANY FURTHER INFORMATION ON CASUALTY AND STATE OF ST FINBARR TO INSURANCE STOP ALSO ADVISE WHETHER SERVICES OF SALVAGE TUG FROM HALIFAX WOULD ASSIST' – TRAWLER**

TO BOWRING, ST JOHN'S AT 2015, 25/12

'WE HAVE REPORT FROM OFFICER IN CHARGE CARTWRIGHT RADIO THAT ST FINBARR IS ON FIRE OFF COAST LABRADOR STOP PLEASE PASS ALL DETAILS TO INSURANCE – URGENT' – TRAWLER

RECEIVED FROM BOWRING ST JOHN (REF V2045) HANDED IN 1650 25/12 READ 1225 26/12

'SUBJECT TO THE CORRECTION FOR NUMBER OF WORDS – FOLLOWING RECEIVED FROM O.I.C. CARTWRIGHT MARINE RADIO 25TH FOLLOWING DISTRESS MESSAGES RECEIVED FROM "SIR FRED PARKES" AT 25.0840 GMT ST FINBARR QFXU ON FIRE POSITION 55 15 W 55 45 N TEN MEN RESCUED TWO MEN LOST THIRTEEN UNACCOUNTED FOR AS OF 1200 GMT VESSEL "SIR FRED PARKES "08CE AND "ORSINO" 05JA STANDING BY AND ATTEMPTING RESCUE OF REMAINING MEN'

---

* Source: The papers of the Hamlings of Hull trawler company lodged at the Hull History Centre archive.

** 'Trawler' was the owners/insurers' telegram signature. Bowring was the St John's-based agent for Hamlings. Source: Hamlings Papers, housed at the Hull History Centre.

CHAPTER TEN

The Hull Daily Mail newsroom.

The reporters' desks faced the newsdesk where a team of four news editors processed copy, dished out orders, answered phones and talked from the sides of their mouths, like bad ventriloquists, with lit cigarettes dangling from their lips. Phone receivers cradled like violins as they scribbled Teeline shorthand with one hand and flicked through copy paper that chronicled everything from Women's Institute coffee mornings to murder with the other. This was the final stop for the news before the sub-editors' desk, the horse-shoe-shaped table diagonally opposite, where the subs each sat in a captain's chair. The chief-sub editor, like the Father, had his deputy at His right hand and chief photographer to His left.

Everyone on that newsroom floor, even the editor, knew that it was the chief sub's world and that He just let them live there. The paper-production Trinity sat on the bend of the U-shaped table and issued commands to the down-table subs either side. Copy was knocked into shape by mostly irascible, often high-functioning alcoholic middle-aged men, whose nerves strained almost as much as their midriff shirt buttons as they ensured properly written, legally safe, clear and interesting copy was delivered to the case room with headlines that fitted.

In the case room, rows of Linotype operators typed in copy that dropped lead letter by lead letter into type galleys (cases) that would make up the paper's content. Typesetters read upside down to spot anything missed by subs, literally minding the *ps* and *qs* – ensuring they were the right way up. The final line of defence – the stone sub-editor – checked proofed pages before they were sent "off stone" – i.e. to the huge presses that for almost a century daily shook the building that housed this great port city newspaper. Men in rows of stools sat in front of those giant ninety-character keyboards, where usually type was set one character at a time to fit perfectly on to the page. Journalists and printers use many terms derived from the days when mostly only monks wrote; for example, the typeface is a font, a workplace for printers (and journalists) a chapel. Shop stewards are called Fathers of Chapel.

The jargon even gave the editor his nickname 'His Nibs', later used in common parlance as a euphemism for bosses in general. It derived from the fact that bygone monastic scribes were among the few who read and wrote; the possessors of pens.

In this place where holy nomenclature proliferated, words were heard that were never seen in The Bible, delivered at top volume above a constant cacophony – and they ensured readers got their news six days a week, right on time, across four editions.

But that Christmas Day the newsroom was a dead place. Phones rang unanswered. There was not even a duty reporter. There would be no paper that day, the next – or the one after. The holiday fell on a Sunday and the print unions ensured an extra day off for its members when holidays came on what would have been statutory time off.

Hull would have to wait for the news.

There was no din, no clouds of fag smoke, no burning cigarette butts in the brass ashtrays bolted to the desks, none of the anger, shouting, swearing and fighting it took to get a newspaper on to the streets after which buzzed newspapermen repaired to the boozers to mark another edition. It was eerily quiet. The only sound was from the case room where the "creed" clicked and buzzed. The creed was another name of religious origin, given to the international newswire that printed out telexed dispatches from the great press agencies of the world. It was so named because it was always believed.

That day, like any other 364, the creed spewed page upon page into its big wire basket – a scene repeated the world over. Normally, these were checked regularly and taken to the newsdesk via a hatch in the wall that linked to the newsroom, to be examined. In that big wire basket stock prices, tide times, war reports, stories of political intrigue, poverty, pain and hope; in short, the world's news, via the Press Association (PA) Wire Service, just kept piling up. More copy was on the floor than in the basket. Somewhere in the pile on the linoleum tiled floor was a PA RUSH (a breaking news bulletin), which in usual circumstances would have sparked the frenzy that heralded a new front page.

It read: 'BRITISH TRAWLER ST FINBARR ABLAZE IN NEWFOUNDLAND'S GRAND BANKS – STOP – EXPLOSION REPORTED – MANY FEARED DEAD – MORE FOLLOWS LATER. STOP.'

The pile of news telex papers under which it lay grew by the hour. That bulletin was there unseen until the day after Boxing Day.

Richard Taylor's house.

Jill Harrison sat with baby Jane on her knee, waiting for the right moment to tell her mum and dad that she was expecting again. She had sent her coded telegram to Tony. She hoped he had got it OK. There had been no ship-to-shore calls.

But now it was time to let everyone else know her good news. Tony would be home after the holidays, and after all, it should be a lot easier this time, she thought. Dad had grown to like Tony. He even bought him a carry-out for the last trip because the lad was skint.

It had been a lovely Christmas morning. Dad had picked her and the bairn up from their little house in Holly Villas, Flinton Grove, off Hessle Road, in his new big Zephyr and taken them to his new house in Gower Road in west Hull.

With all the friends and family milling about there, she just never seemed to get the chance to get Mam or Dad to herself. Each time she had plucked up the courage, fate got in the way. The posh new living room was very cosy with its real coal fire roaring in the grate. Dad had backed it up and it gave off a fierce heat, so much so that Mam warned the gang of hyper kids who came to visit to stay away from the fireguard, which was almost as hot as the grate.

'You've overdone it wi' that fire, you Richard,' Mam admonished.

'Don't be so daft, lass,' Richard replied dismissively.

There was a knock at the door. It was one of the new neighbours. From the living room Jill and her mam could hear Richard talking with the man at the door.

'Are you sure?'

'Aye, come and look. You'll probably need to be getting fire brigade.'

Mam and Jill, with the baby in her arms, joined the two men at the front of the house. It was very clear that the Taylors' chimney was well and truly ablaze.

'Shall I phone the fire brigade?'

'No lass, I'll deal with it mesen. No need for fire engines. It's Christmas Day. I don't want to be wasting their time.'

With that, he thanked his new neighbour and headed for the shed to get his ladder and some bags of sand.

Dad was soon on the roof dropping sand down the chimney. In the living room Mam was dampening down the coal.

'I'll tell them later,' thought Jill. There were quite a few folks in the house. Mam was cooking duck and a turkey. The table was fit for a visiting diplomat. It was a kind of double celebration – a family Christmas and a housewarming – quite literally now, given the chimney fiasco.

Kids were bustling. Toys were scattered around. Dad rested in his armchair after his chimney stack exertions. The telly was off, much to the kids' chagrin, as it always was in the Taylor house when they entertained. In common with most in their circles the Taylors considered it the height of bad manners to have the TV on while guests visited. Dinner was about an hour away. Jill thought maybe she would talk to Mam and Dad before, if she got just the right moment.

Her reverie was shattered by her mother's scream.

Jill, Dad and younger son Rob were in the kitchen in seconds. On the floor lay a massive roasting tray. It was ablaze. A duck and a turkey and stuffing was scattered around it. Dad put out the flames while Rob and Jill helped Mam pick up the food using towels. Rob stood guard at the kitchen to keep the kids out. It was obvious Mam had suffered some burns to her arms. She looked for the Germolene in the cupboard below the sink.

Dad said, 'What the heck happened? You ok, love?'

Mam applied her ointment and replied, 'I don't know. I just went to fetch birds from the oven and it all just burst into flames. Fat must've caught fire, I guess.'

After the kerfuffle of the chimney and the fiery birds, dinner went ahead. Jill decided she'd wait to tell them about the new bairn, maybe when there was not so much going on.

After dinner, Jill, her sister-in-law and one of the other girls helped Mam put away the dishes and generally tidied up. One of the lads still at the table handed over a full ashtray to the girl. It had a flickering stub in among the mass of butts.

'Watch it wi' that ashtray, what wi' today's goings-on. You know what they about things happening in threes, eh?' the girl said.

'Aye, that's all we need... another bloody fire drama,' Dad added.[1]

Alan Burgin was full of Christmas spirit as he made his way up Hull's Spring Bank. He had had a few pints with his mates and was walking to the new council estate at Longhill. It was a mild day for the time of year so a walk would do him good, he thought – plus he'd be sober by the time he reached his mam's house. She would be keen to see him. She always was since he moved out earlier that year. She was also on her own as Alan's siblings were away. Kid brother Robert was in the Army and his elder sister Pauline was married and living out of town. More importantly, Dad was at sea.

Alan's mam always worried when Dad was at sea. This, coupled with being alone at Christmas, compelled the twenty-two-year-old to check his mother was coping. She suffered from "her nerves" and had a life-limiting lung disease. Dad was not due back until well into January. Alan missed his old man.

The old fella was not a big drinker but always took Alan out for a pint or two when home and the lad never had to put his hand in his pocket. Unusually on the last trip his dad took booze with him to sea. Maybe because it was a new ship, the son thought. Just before Jack went back to sea they had talked about getting the pub at Patrington.

Alan had laughed it off – at first. But his old man was deadly serious and told the lad he was going on the new stern trawler to make some extra cash and it would be his last trip.

Dad had said that loads of times before. Secretly, Alan hoped he did mean it because he had told the boy that he would be a cook in the new venture. More importantly, it would be a restful place for Mam. Alan's dad had always looked out for Alan's mam for as long as the boy could remember. That's what his mam needed – peace, quiet and fresh air.

Jack Smith was Alan's stepdad, but Alan never thought of him in that way. He was the only father he had ever known and they were very close. Jack was the father Alan Burgin would have chosen.

He had known nothing but kindness from easy-going Jack, who took Alan, his kid brother and his elder sister as his own the day he married Joan, some twenty years after their biological father, Harold Burgin, an itinerant entertainer from Sheffield, deserted them.

Alan set off for Longhill Estate with thoughts of his dad. For some reason, his mind went back to one of his mam's confinements some fifteen years earlier.

He remembered how Dad took him and his two siblings to Hull Royal Infirmary only to be told children were not allowed on to the ward.

They managed just to glimpse their pleurisy-stricken mam for a few seconds. Dad went back to the corridor with them, sat them down and said, 'Don't worry, kids, I'll just have a word wi' yer mam and we'll sort it out.' Twenty minutes later Jack and his three kids were sitting on the low perimeter wall outside on Prospect Street over which the old Victorian hospital towered.

'Look up,' said Jack.

The three kids craned their necks.

'Can you see her, then?'

The kids spotted their mam waving from her ward window.

That became the family's visiting routine for the duration of Joan's stay. It was that sort of thing that made Alan Burgin love the man he called Dad.

It was about 5.30pm when Alan arrived at 7, Ellingham Close, Longhill Estate. There was enough food on the buffet table to feed a party of twenty. There was only she and Alan in the lounge. The boy made himself at home. The pair exchanged gifts and settled in to watch telly. Alan wanted to watch a film on the independent channel.

'We'll turn it over after the news. I haven't seen the news all day and there's no papers. Have to keep up, don't we?' Joan quipped.

Alan was quite surprised by his mother's jocular mood. She wasn't one for the quip. She was usually on edge. Maybe the couple of glasses of Bailey's had had the desired effect. He went to the kitchenette for a beer while his mam turned on the TV set in the corner. It usually took a minute or so to warm up, so Alan helped himself from the buffet table and then the fridge. From the kitchen, he heard a sharp scream followed by a crash. Alan rushed back to the lounge.

His mother was lying passed-out on the carpet. The contents of her Bailey's glass spilled around her like blood from a head wound. On the flickering, black and white TV screen, Alan saw a still, captioned, photograph of a stern trawler. '…and we will bring more about the fate of the Hull ship's crew when we get it,' completed the announcer's report. He sat down next to his mother and began to bring her round.[2]

Twenty miles away, a telephone call was taken at a grand country house that was once home to a man who changed England's history. That call would change the lives of twenty-five Hull fishing families.

Scorborough Hall was at the heart of its community. Farm workers, villagers and estate employers had been at the Christmas service at the church on the house's grounds and returned home to enjoy the remains of the day.

The Hall, in its differing reincarnations, had been there for more than 800 years. Its most famous residents were Sir John Hotham (1589-1645) and his son, also John Hotham (1610-1645). Hotham senior was the son of John Hotham, High Sheriff of Yorkshire. He served in the Thirty Years War and sat as MP for Beverley during the reign of Charles I. He was knighted in 1617 and became the first baronet on January 14, 1622. The first resident was William de Hotham (c.1100-1166).

On January 11, 1642, Charles I appointed the Earl of Newcastle as Governor of Hull and Parliament appointed Sir John Hotham, who believed he held the town in the "King's authority signified by the Lords and Commons in Parliament".

Old Sir John did not quite see it that way. This became a problem when the King demanded entry to Hull on April 23, 1642, an act that sparked the English Civil War. Hotham refused him entry on the grounds it would betray his commission to keep the town secure. He was declared a traitor. He and his eldest son were executed on consecutive days at the beginning of January 1645.

The house burned down in 1705, and the family moved to South Dalton, a nearby East Yorkshire village. A new

Scorborough Hall was built on the site in the early to mid-18th century and boasted its own lake, woods, fifty-metre fishpond and parish church – St Leonard's – all on its moated grounds. So many trees surrounded it, that even in winter when all the leaves had fallen, the Hall was still shrouded from view.[3]

Jonathan Watson Hall had been called from the Christmas dinner table to take a call in his study there.

'Jonathan, it's Jack Ellis.'

The young man listened intently as Ellis, the shipping manager, told him how their super-ship was ablaze, under tow, and twelve of the *St Finbarr*'s crew were unaccounted for.

'I'll take care of everything this end, Jonathan,' Ellis continued. 'Bowrings (the Canadian agents) have everything in hand. We know there are casualties but not who or how many.

'The ship's still ablaze and being towed by the *Orsino* doing a steady five knots. But you need to be there, make sure the men get all they need, make whatever arrangements we might need. If there's more to tell, I will let you know. Call me when you get to the airport.'

'Yes, yes, of course,' said Jonathan as he scribbled down details on the large notepad on top of the leather-covered desk. On automatic pilot, he set about finding his passport and getting packed for the trip. Less than an hour later Jonathan's Wolseley Six sped down the long, winding cinder path from the Hall on to the main A165, and headed for London. Ellis had booked him on a flight to St John's, Newfoundland, via Montreal.

*Royal Mission to Deep Sea Fishermen, Goulton Street,
off Hessle Road. 7pm.*

David MacMillan was exhausted. It had been a very tiring but worthwhile couple of days for the Superintendent of the Royal Mission to Deep Sea Fishermen for Hull, but he was looking forward to what was left of his family's Christmas. The tall, bespectacled clergyman was tidying his desk. He picked up the paper hat left over from that day's Mission lunch, scrunched it and threw it into the waste basket.

'That's it for another year,' he thought. The past forty-eight hours could not have been busier or more varied. Saturday, Christmas Eve, was the party for the widows and orphans, those families in hardship and basically anyone with children who needed it. From one o' clock until three was taken up by screeching kids whom even lunch could not quieten. That was followed by games and presents from a visiting Father Christmas (at least there was no shortage of big old men with white beards in the fishing community). The day was all you would expect from four hours of kids full of food, sweets and excitement.

Next day it was the turn of the old men – and some younger ones with nowhere to go – to mark the birth of their Saviour. The Mission hosted a lunch each year for the old and lonely who had sailed in times past, those who were alone in Christmas present – and any stranded foreign sailors in port. Inmates of the Queens Hostel, the Salvation Army and the other local model lodging houses were also welcomed to dine alongside the men who lived in the

Mission's spartan rooms. Now the office was quiet, the hall outside tidied and MacMillan was ready to enjoy the remainder of the festive season.

The phone rang.

The clergyman assumed it was his wife, wanting to know when he would be back up to the flat. He picked it up with a breezy, 'Hello!'

'It's Claude here, David.'

MacMillan could tell by his tone it was not good news. The Fishing Industry Welfare Officer for Hull, Claude A Weissenborn, told the young clergyman about the telegrams received from the owners, and about the men still unaccounted for.

'We don't know much. The *Orsino*'s there with the *Sir Fred Parkes*. We simply don't know who is dead or alive. I'll draw up the crew list and come and join you soon, David. I know it's a big ask on Christmas Day but I suggest you get as many volunteers as you can.'

David listened carefully and replied, 'But we don't know anything other than there's a ship ablaze and some men may not be alive.'

'I know, but at least we can try to offer some comfort. They're all in the dark. We had better get to them before they hear something on television or the wireless, or worse if they hear gossip from the pubs. I think the BBC has put something out, but it's so inconclusive it's had just made things worse. There's no newspapers until Wednesday. So, we need to get out there. We might learn more soon.'

'Very well, Claude. I'll see you soon. It's going to be a long night.'[4]

Rayner's Bar, Hessle Road. Near closing time.

'In't your Jill's fella on that ship?'

'What?'

'The *St Finbarr*.'

Jill's younger brother, Rob Taylor, could only hear every second word. The bar was mobbed. Christmas night in Rayner's always was. He was with a big gang of fisher lads. The longest bar in Hull was heaving. The dozens of pints of mild with vodka and lime chasers did not help. Rob did not quite recognise the lad who tried to talk to him. He knew he was a fisher lad and had seen him around Road.

'You what?' Rob repeated.

The lad beckoned him to the doorway.

The din became background noise as the pair stepped out.

Rob's stomach heaved as the lad talked.

'It's that new stern trawler *St Finbarr*. It's afire. They think there's some lads are dead. One of me mates is a sparks and he heard the ship's being towed on the Grand Banks wi' some dead lads still aboard.'

Rob did not know what to say. He thought of his sister at home. What should he do? It was all rumour.

Deep down Rob knew there could be something in what the fisher lad said. He just did not want to believe it. Telegram traffic from trawlers did not stay private for long. There was always an office worker who overheard or newly landed sparks with a tale, or rather half of one, to tell. The community knew that the Hessle Road jungle telegraph was always first with the news. He was trying to take in what the lad had said when his gang of mates spilled out on Road and he went further out with them.

He thanked the fisher lad, straightened himself, and set off to catch up with his pals. He was scared and worried. If it was right, she should know, but if it was wrong it would worry the whole family sick. Rob did not know what to do.

He and his mates drifted past Flinton Street, where his sister lived. He thought about going down there but remembered that Jill was at Dad's house. He glanced down the terraces briefly and walked on.

'C'mon, soft lad, keep up!' one of the gang shouted.

'Yeah right, coming,' Rob shouted back and decided he would not go home that night.[5] Fewer than two hundred yards away David MacMillan knocked on a door in Holly Villas, off Flinton Street. He knew it was where Jill Harrison lived. There was no reply. He rapped on the door loudly. An old lady from across the way shouted to him.

'They're not in, Reverend. They've gone to her dad's.'

'Do you know where?'

'No, sorry, Reverend. They used to be on St George's Road but they've moved up Boothferry way. Is everything all right, Reverend?'

'Yes, madam. We've just got to check something with her,' MacMillan replied.

'You could try their Billy's,' the old lady said, pointing to the terrace across the road.

MacMillan and one of his colleagues crossed over to Jill's older brother's front door as the old lady fixed them in her stare from the other pavement.

MacMillan rapped on the door with that authoritative knock many in the community knew and dreaded.

There was no reply. A cursory glance through the living room window confirmed there was no-one at home. The terrace front came straight on the pavement. There was no garden or front yard, so it was very easy to check if someone was at home – a boon for many a frustrated rent collector.

Billy Taylor and his family were away visiting his in-laws for the holiday. MacMillan looked at the paper attached to the clipboard in his hand and then went back across the way to his waiting Morris Minor, gunned the little engine and set off to the next house on the crew list.

FROM BOXING DAY RADIO/TELEGRAM TRAFFIC*

TELEGRAM RECEIVED FROM MASTER, SIR FRED PARKES, HANDED IN 1545 26/12 WICK RECEIVED 1610 26.12,

'ONLY ASSISTED DURING RESCUE OF SURVIVORS STOP ORSINO TOOK VESSEL IN TOW LAST NIGHT STILL ON FIRE AND STILL PROCEEDING ST JOHN'S NO FURTHER INFORMATION SUGGEST CONTACT ORSINO'

TELEGRAM SENT TO MASTER, 'SIR FRED PARKES' AT 1630 26/12:

'YOUR MESSAGE HANDED IN 1545 26/12 RECEIVED CAN YOU CONFRIM THAT YOU HAVE NO SURVIVORS ON SIR FRED PARKES' – TRAWLER**

TELEGRAM SENT TO MASTER, 'ORSINO' AT 16 00 26/12:

'DO YOU KNOW WHAT HAPPENED TO REMAINDER OF CREW STOP DID THEY GET AWAY FROM ST FINBARR STOP IF NO HAVE CANADIAN RESCUE SERVICE BEEN IN OPERATION' – TRAWLER**

TELEGRAM RECEIVED FROM 'ORSINO' HANDED IN 1730 26/12 RECEIVED 1815 26/12

'HAVE ST FINBARR STILL IN TOW STOP ON BOARD THIRTEEN SURVIVORS NAMES AS FOLLOWS: T. SAWYER W. COLLIER, H. WILLIAMS, E. SAMMS, T. HARDWICK, G. GRINLAW, H. PRINCE, D. WHITTAKER, A. EVANS, V. BULL, E. PETRINI, J. SCOTT, P. TOGNOLA, STOP ALSO THE BODY OF H. SMITH STOP MEMBERS OF CREW MISSING: K. PULLEN, R. MATTHEWS, J. HAMILTON, A. HARRISON, G. ODELL, J. SIGURRDSSON, J. SMITH, T. GRAY, D. YOUNG, S. BRIGHAM, R. COULMAN' – SIGNED WOOLDRIDGE**

TELEGRAM RECEIVED FROM 'ORSINO' HANDED IN 1945 26/12 RECEIVED 2015 26/12,

** TEN MEN WERE TRAPPED IN ACCOMMODATION ST. FINBARR STOP TWO MEN LOST SCALING ABOARD ORSINO STOP ONE BODY RECOVERED – SIGNED SAWYER**

TELEGRAM RECEIVED FROM SKIPPER CURTIS OF THE 'SIR FRED PARKES': PORTISHEAD 1700

RECEIVED 1925

'REGRET WE HAVE NO SURVIVORS ON BOARD'

---

* Source: The papers of the Hamlings of Hull trawler company lodged at the Hull History Centre archive.

CHAPTER ELEVEN

Boxing Day, 2am, The Mission offices, Hull.

The two-bar electric heater at the foot of his desk offered an orange glow but little other comfort for David MacMillan. His Crombie coat was soaked after hours of trudging house to house. A few years earlier this task would have been completed in two-to-three hours but the new-build estates on the city boundaries had attracted a diaspora of Hessle Roaders, whose homes had been demolished in slum clearances.

He slumped into his office chair, head in hands, elbows on his desk. He took off his horn-rimmed spectacles, rubbed his tired eyes and drifted into thought.

A small, disc-shaped pool of light from the angle-poise lit part of the green leather surface of his desktop. The clergyman was exhausted. He thought of the dozens of people whose yuletide he and his team had shattered with uncertainties unleashed by the limited, sketchy news of the *St Finbarr*. He marvelled at the volunteers who had been with him, and shuddered when he remembered how the parties-in-full-swing became freeze-frame tableaux as folk opened their door to the Man from the Mission.

Sadder still, MacMillan wondered if he had done any good with his incomplete missives. He felt a poor harbinger indeed. He told himself it was better they were prepared – and maybe comforted – by him and his team than having dealt alone with a surprise view of a news broadcast, or worse, hearing gossip with which the community was abuzz.

Every Hessle Roader knows somebody who is a radio operator, or works at the shipping offices, only too ready to spread half-baked, often exaggerated news. MacMillan must have concluded that the most he had done for the families he had visited last night was to ensure they had as little sleep as he. The Mission Man was desperate to put their minds at rest. He expected to have known more but the Hamlings shipping manager Jack Ellis said severe weather and atrocious atmospheric conditions meant rescue trawlers could not be readily contacted. The airways were also cluttered by Christmas messages to ships at sea from across the world.

Telephone links to Labrador were overloaded and there were two-and-a-half-hour delays, even for emergency calls. The truth was that very little was known.[1] He was disappointed that he was not able to find Jill Harrison's family and hoped that she and her family had not seen the brief, devastating, incomplete BBC bulletin – or worse still –fallen victim to gossip from the Hessle Road jungle telegraph.

MacMillan would be back at his desk in fewer than six hours, ready again to deliver heartache or relief for twenty-five confused, frightened families. Just as well the clergyman "lived above the shop" – he would not have far to go to rest.

He and his curate Donald Woolley had family quarters amid the dormitories and rooms where those in need were housed. There was also the small matter of putting on Boxing Day lunches later for stranded foreign sailors, old ex-fishermen and others with nowhere else to go, dependent on Christian charity. MacMillan told himself that the staff and volunteers would have to cope without him. It was going to be a long day.

Boxing Day, 0730hours, 50 miles off Newfoundland.

Two deckhands were at the rail having a smoke on the German trawler the *MT Hamburg*. Like dozens of other ships in the area she had gone earlier to help the *St Finbarr* and was still on standby – but the English seemed to have things in hand. They could see the *St Finbarr* being towed stern first by the rescue ship. It was a couple of miles away at most. The two German deckhands could see the palls of smoke still rising from the wheelhouse. The ship bow was partly submerged. The towing was slow.

The rescue ship *Orsino* could not be doing more than five knots. The pair were not particularly looking at anything as their ship rose and fell on the swell. Around them the sea was slowly swirling. Other shipping around was appearing and reappearing on the waves and troughs. The horizon of steel-grey swollen sea seemed to meld into the gunmetal-hue of the horizon. One of the men pointed and nudged his shipmate. 'Look,' he said, 'there – on the swell.'

'What is it?' the other replied.

'I hope I'm wrong, my friend, but I think it's a man.'

The pair strained to see. There was something there and, whatever it was, not much of it was above the water. Normally, if a man was spotted there would be a brightly coloured lifejacket. Whatever they were looking at seemed almost to merge into the colours of the sea. There was no lifejacket.

The two men continued to look out towards the figure when a wave rose it from the water briefly before it submerged again. There was now no doubt about what was in the water just yards out from the ship.

'I think we'd better fetch the captain.'

Half an hour later, on the bridge of the *Orsino,* skipper Wooldridge was interrupted when radio man Bill Dunn came in.

'Boss, you'd better come through to the wireless room.'

Once there, Dunn said, 'Skipper, it looks like they've found one of the *Finbarr* lads. I didn't want to speak with men being on the bridge.'

'You do right, Bill. How was he found?'

'It was a German trawler, the *Hamburg.* They've pulled a fella from the water and they're on their way to us.'[2]

Boxing Day, 0730hours, The Royal Mission to
Deep Sea Fishermen, Hull.

MacMillan had not slept much. He had washed, shaved and breakfasted. He always made sure he had a full breakfast, for sometimes that would be the only time he would eat in a day. It was only five hours since he was last there.

He heard the loud *Brrinng! Brrinng!* of the big black telephone on his oak desk as he unlocked his office door. His left arm was still in its jacket sleeve as the other lifted the receiver from its cradle. He swapped the receiver to his other hand and removed his jacket. He draped it over the chair.

'I'm sorry… I… you'll have to calm down. Please, speak slowly…'

MacMillan struggled to calm the hysterical female caller.

'I don't know any more than I did yesterday. If there's any more, be assured we will get the news to you first…'

The owner of the screeching voice was not listening and was barely comprehensible.

'Now, Mrs…? … Can you please just give me your name…? I can't help if I don't know who you are.'

'You were in me 'ouse last night, Reverend,' the voice said between heavy sobs.

'I was in many houses last night. Now, please… calm… please…'

The *burrrr…* tone told the clergyman the call was over.

'She just hung up!' MacMillan said out loud to no-one.

'Grief gets them like that sometimes, David,' said a voice from the doorway.

MacMillan looked up. It was Claude Weissenborn. He had a mug of tea in each hand.

'You look like you'll need one of these, David.' Weissenborn placed the mugs on two silver coasters. He pulled up a seat and lifted his cup.

'That phone has been ringing constantly for ages. I've been here an hour – and the cleaner told me it had been going off before that.'

MacMillan reached for his tea.

The phone rang again.

'Hello, David MacMillan…'

The pattern was set for the day.

Boxing Day 0830hours, off Newfoundland.

Two deckhands lowered an empty life raft over the side of the *Orsino* on a very long line and fed it out toward the German ship headed alongside. *Orsino* crewmen and some from the *St Finbarr* milled around and watched. The life raft bobbed further and further away toward the *MT Hamburg* as she manoeuvred into the little craft's path.

From the bridge, skipper Wooldridge could see a few of the German crew at the rail. They lowered a line that was then attached to the raft. The men pulled the raft towards their vessel and further secured it.

Another man descended a ladder, the bottom of which was alongside the raft. He drew level with it, leaned and opened the flaps, then clung back to the ladder.

Above the ladder-man, a tarpaulin-wrapped body was lowered gently on a winch. Minutes later, the ladder-man guided it into the raft, secured the flaps and returned to the rail where his comrades pulled him over and on to the deck.[3]

The *Orsino* men pulled the loaded raft back. Bosun George Patrick oversaw the men who pulled on the line until the raft was close enough to be hoisted by winch. The body was landed on the deck as gently as was possible.

'Get back. Give us some room. Show some respect, lads.' The crewmen near the tarp stepped back, leaving two deckhands and the bosun to do their work.

Bosun Patrick untied the top of the cloth and pulled the tarpaulin partly open. A sharp intake of breath followed as he recognised his old pal Curly Smith. Up in the wheelhouse, skipper Wooldridge continued battling towards St John's with the blazing *St Finbarr* in tow. The weather took another turn for the worse and he was fighting a strong northerly gale.

Wooldridge could not get his ship above four knots. The powerful engines strained as they pulled the 1,139-ton blazing ship and her 400-ton cargo to which was added the unknown weight of the water that had sunk the bow of the *St Finbarr*.

Time taken bringing Curly Smith's body aboard compounded the delay too. The 100 or so miles to St John's seemed a long, long way. Initially the owners advised the *Orsino* headed for St Anthony, which had better medical facilities for catastrophic injuries.

Wooldridge decided to go for the other port which was 110 miles nearer. The *St Finbarr* men mainly suffered frostbite, exposure and swollen legs, all of which the *Orsino's* commander knew could be dealt with at St John's.

The skipper kept at the wheel, quietly determined to land the *St Finbarr* and her crew, living and dead. Wooldridge must have wondered what could come next. From the first minute that he had answered Tommy Sawyer's SOS, a series of setbacks had been overcome. The skilled helmsman was in his final leg of the voyage. He would go head-in to the burgeoning gale. Four knots would have to do.

At least they were moving and the *St Finbarr*, although bow-first in the water, stayed afloat on the stern-first tow.

On the *Orsino* two deckhands armed with large, sharp axes guarded the towline, ready in an instant to cut through the warps should the blazing ship start to sink. Steady Eddie Wooldridge lived up to his nickname, kept his cool and ensured his ship, coupled to her crippled, blazing charge, edged ever closer to land.

In the *Orsino* engine room the needles on the dials that registered the torque of the ship's motor dropped. Fast. The *Orsino* suddenly was free to speed up. Her engines had to be made to relent. A rumble proceeded the sudden changes. The engineers realised immediately what had happened.

The two axe-armed deckhands standing by the warp realised at the same time. In the wheelhouse, Wooldridge took a message from engine room. What he was told did not surprise him. Stood next to him was mate Lee.

'Bryan, the towline has snapped. We must get back aboard the *Finbarr* and try to get it reconnected. We can't give up now. We're nearly there.'

There was a hint of desperation in the normally uber-calm skipper's voice.

Lee looked out the window and said, 'It cannot be done right now, skipper. The wind's too high and it's still too dark. We'll have to wait until it clears a bit.' Lee was not keen to return to the stricken ship, but knew there was no other option.

'Let's hope she's still afloat when it does, Bryan. She's nose-down in the water.'

The Mission Hall, Hull, Boxing Day, afternoon.

Goulton Street's Mission to Deep Fishermen was deluged all day with calls and even visits from relatives desperate for news. All that was known was that the *St Finbarr* was ablaze and that about half the crew had been accounted for. There was also a rumour that another Hull trawler, the *Sir Fred Parkes,* had some of the *St Finbarr* men aboard.

MacMillan could only tell them that which he knew, which was very little. He tried to keep them calm, told them not to listen to the rumours and to wait for the bosses to confirm the truth. All in vain. Hessle Road's Christmas was shattered, especially for those *St Finbarr* families. MacMillan and his 23-year-old fresh-faced curate, Donald Woolley, kept the lunches going, fed the needy, handed out gifts and tried as much as they could not to let the massive weight of worry get in the way of their work. In the main hall, trestle-tables laden with Christmas fare were surrounded by the flotsam and jetsam of the industry. The old, the stranded, the lonely and the poor who all had one thing in common; none of them had anywhere else to be. They wore paper hats and pulled the crackers and gratefully received the Christian hospitality from the busy volunteers.

Most of the guests were fishermen or ex-fishermen. They too knew of the unfolding *St Finbarr* tragedy and the rumours that it had brought to hang over Hessle Road like a darkening, enveloping sea fog. The clergyman told them all he could, kept them informed but he felt increasingly stressed and powerless. They had to just wait and see.

MacMillan became increasingly listless. He headed back into his office and lifted his now-dried Crombie coat from the back of his chair. Once his coat was on he walked into the hall to speak with his curate.

'Donald, it's David. I am going out for a while. Can you look after things? Shouldn't be more than hour. I am just popping out to see if I can find Jill Harrison.'

'Of course,' replied the curate.

MacMillan set off to find the trawlerman's wife whom he had known since she was a baby. He remembered her as a tomboy always trying to muscle into the Mission youth club to play snooker and pool with her brothers and the other lads at the boys-only club.

He recalled the many times he had sent her out from there, but not before she had got her crisps and free pop from the tuck shop. He was not sure how the woman the little girl had become would react. MacMillan set off back to Flinton Grove.

This time, Billy Taylor was at home and minutes later the vicar's Morris Minor was heading for Richard Taylor's house.

Boxing Day, mid-afternoon, Richard Taylor's house.

Jill Harrison was in her element. Despite the chimney fire and the roast tins dramas, Christmas was grand. Now the guests had gone and there was just Mum, Dad, baby Jane, Jill and her bump. Her parents knew they were to be grandparents once more. She could not have given them a better Christmas gift.

In the kitchen Mum was making herself busy. Festive music drifted through from the radio in the living room as Dad rested in his favourite chair. Baby Jane was gurgling and burbling as Jill played with her and bathed her in the little pink freestanding basin that sat atop a metal frame. Each time she squeezed the soapy sponge over the infant's head, the baby giggled. Mum joined in with the bath game but was subdued.

Rob had not returned home, nor had he called to say why. She knew he would probably be sleeping it off at a pal's house and was just thoughtless the way young lads are, but she would feel better when she saw him. A mother's worry is never far away. But she kept herself busy and played with her granddaughter as Jill fetched a fluffy white, warm towel with which to dry the baby.

Mum went into the living room. Jill could hear her ask Dad if he wanted a cup of tea. Jill lifted the baby out of the little tub and patted her down with a towel on the nearby table where a set of fresh clothes lay for little Jane. The firm, loud *rat-tat-tat* carried into the kitchen over the music from the radio.

Jill fleetingly thought she recognised it, but that thought came as quickly as it had come. She carried on drying the baby.

At first, Richard Taylor thought the silhouette behind the frosted glass was that of a policeman. His gut was knotted. A hundred worries flashed through his mind as he fiddled with the door chain. Was this going to be about Rob?

When the door opened, his heart sank.

'Can I come in, Mr Taylor? We have some bad news,' the man said. Richard recognised him as the man from the Mission.

'Yes, of course, Reverend, come in,' Richard said.

MacMillan proffered his hand to be shaken. As he did so another voice drifted in from the living room. It was quiet but had a sense of underlying urgency.

'What is it, Richard? Is it about our Robert?'

Richard replied to his wife, 'No love. It's all right. It's the man from the Mission. Just keep our Jill in the living room.'

Jill held her baby close. Mum came in and asked her to go to the front lounge but Jill could not move. She strained to hear what Mr MacMillan said.

She could not pick up all the conversation but heard enough to make the butterflies flutter in her life-filling belly. *'The ship's ablaze... two men have died in the rescue... we do not know who... the crew are not accounted for... we will know more later... you must not listen to any chit-chat or gossip...'*

Jill was not aware of her mother's arms around her. She heard the clunk of the big front door that followed the farewell exchange between MacMillan and her father. Mum guided her to the living room and gently took the baby from her. Her father was standing. His face was pale and stern.

'Oh, Dad! Has owt happened to my Tony?' Tears rolled down her face.

'They don't know owt, Jill. Just that two lads have been killed and the ship's afire. There's been a rescue. Maybe Tony's wi' them, eh? We'll just have to wait and see.'

Then he added, as if by way of comfort, 'No-one knows owt for sure.'

Jill wept as all around became background noise to the onslaught of overpowering fear and anxiety. She could hear her father's voice but was not listening. Her mind was racing. Phrases ran like telex ticker-tape through her mind. '...*not accounted for... rescue... don't know for sure... ship on fire... men saved...*'

It was a blur. She sat and wept amid the comforting voices, not knowing if her Tony was coming home again, if he was dead or alive, and then she fleetingly felt bad for hoping the victims were someone else's horror, some other girl's love. She could think of nothing other than her Tony.

Outside, the engine of an old Morris Minor rattled and drifted off into the distance. In the living room the radio was turned off.

The Taylors tended to their frightened daughter.

Hamlings offices, 6pm.

Shipping manager Jack Ellis and his deputy Albert Robinson had been on duty most of the day. Telephone lines to Labrador were still down. They could not contact their agents in St John's due to heavy radio traffic and atmospheric interference from the freezing gales and blizzards.

Jonathan Watson Hall, the boss's son, was in St John's and had been in touch with Bowrings (Hamlings' Canadian agents) to prepare for whatever eventuality they may have had to face. There had been no call from Watson Hall that day. Ellis and Robinson were dependent on telegram messages from ships at the scene. Things were not clear. Ellis feared the worst, but hoped for the best. After all, no news is good news, isn't it?

At the dockside office, he read the print-out of the telegram from Lloyd's of London handed to him fresh from the telex just minutes earlier:

TELEGRAM   RECEIVED   FROM   MASTER, SIR   FRED   PARKES,   HANDED   IN   1545 26/12 WICK RECEIVED 1610 26.12, 'ONLY ASSISTED DURING RESCUE OF SURVIVORS STOP ORSINO TOOK VESSEL IN TOW LAST NIGHT STILL ON FIRE AND STILL PROCEEDING ST JOHN'S NO FURTHER INFORMATION SUGGEST CONTACT ORSINO'

The second memo read:

Telegram received from Skipper Curtis of the Sir Fred Parkes: Portishead 1700/Received 1925 'REGRET WE HAVE NO SURVIVORS ON BOARD.'4

Ellis turned to Robinson and said, 'Bert, best try to get on to Eddie Wooldridge on the *Orsino* and find out the score. It doesn't sound good.'

The Mission Hall.

It was about seven in the evening when the last stragglers left and the guests were settled in the recreation area or their own berths. MacMillan and his team set about cleaning up in between the calls that still came in. He had been back from the Taylors' house for about three hours. Through all that time the phone calls had not stopped and had been fielded by Donald, MacMillan and others in turn. By 7.30pm Mac-Millan's patience was at its limit. He took to his office and took the phone off the hook.

'Just for a few minutes,' he thought. 'Just need to think. A few minutes' peace to think.'

He sat quietly in meditation. But his mind could not rest. He could not let the phone stay off its cradle.

He replaced it. Minutes later, the loud ring shattered the quiet of the office and startled the vicar. He picked up the receiver and gave out a sharp, un-vicar-like, 'Yes...!'

His tone changed just as quickly. It was Claude Weissenborn.

'David, we have the full story and it's not good. Ten men dead aboard the *St Finbarr* after an explosion. Thirteen survivors on the *Orsino*. Two men were lost in the rescue.

'That's all that has been confirmed from Hamlings. I'll be over shortly with the crew list of those who have perished. Twelve families in all, David.'

The burr that followed Claude hanging up buzzed through MacMillan's brain as he struggled with the enormity of the task ahead of him. He replaced the receiver, said a quiet prayer and prepared to go back to work. It was 8pm when he and his team took to the streets to break bad news to city's unluckiest twelve families and good news to the lucky thirteen.

It was always the bad news first.

In the East Yorkshire village of Cottingham, north of the city, the *Hull Daily Mail*'s news editor Charles Levitt enjoyed the rare privilege of another relatively stress-free day. There was no paper until the twenty-eighth. The thirty-six-year-old, slim-built, sandy-haired journalist had determined to enjoy the festive time with his family and the extra day off that came from Christmas falling on a Sunday.

Like all newspapermen he knew there was no such thing as a guaranteed day off. A thousand things could send a news reporter to work at a moment's notice. The best of news journalists recognises these moments in an instant. That's news sense. It can be sparked by a varied host of things: a phone call, an incident on the street, a snippet overheard in the pub, even a fact that leaps from a dry-as-dust council report.

The more highly tuned the news sense, the better the reporter. Those on his paper who possessed it had already called him after hearing the BBC snippet, to be thanked and told the matter was in hand. But Levitt knew those men would be in early on what would have been a day off. News outlets of all kinds depend on those with this ability and enthusiasm. Old newspapermen used to say, 'If I have to explain what it is, you ain't got it, kid.'

Well, Charles Levitt had it in spades. His youthful appearance belied the fact he was a twenty-year veteran of local newspapers, having started as a sixteen-year-old on a weekly paper in Wisbech, Cambridgeshire. Just after eight o'clock that evening that hard-earned skill was tested when the hallway phone rang. The newsman lifted the receiver.

'Levitt.'

'Hello, Charles. It's Bob.'

Levitt recognised the gravelly Aussie accent as that of Robert S Wellings, the paper's docklands diarist and shipping correspondent, who had made his home in Hull just after the Second World War. The ex-ANZAC anglophile's voice was one made from thousands of Capstan Full Strength cigarettes, St Bruno pipe tobacco and fine malt whisky. Levitt sat at the telephone table-cum-stool, lifted the notebook and one of the many pencils that always were near the phone. He automatically cradled the receiver violin-style, and started taking notes. He had been expecting this call since the conversation he had with Wellings after the BBC put out the incomplete, unhelpful bulletin on Christmas night.

The two men spoke and Wellings told his boss he'd get on the case ASAP. Levitt knew that Robert S Wellings, unlike the Beeb, was never brief nor incomplete about anything – and when he did call back it would be with the whole story. Nothing happened on the docks that Wellings did not know about; he often found out before the dock workers, fishermen and bobbers who worked there did. He would have phoned a few contacts and a few called him.

The news editor's Teeline shorthand filled page after page as Wellings reported in. The docklands reporter had heard from a few sources that the *St Finbarr* was ablaze, ten men were dead aboard and two had been lost. He knew there were thirteen survivors aboard the rescue ship. He told his boss nobody knew what had caused the big fire aboard. There were rumours of an electrical fire or an explosion, but Wellings was confident he would know more soon. In the meantime, he had a copy of the crew list of those who had perished and those who survived.

'The Mission folk are out now seeing the bereaved families,' Wellings continued.

'I'll deal with Hamlings and Dasher Ellis and work on a backgrounder. Tell the subs' desk to expect a load early doors. They'll have to stitch it all together.'

'Thanks, Bob,' said Levitt. 'We best let the Mission men get on with their work tonight. I will send a team out on the knock tomorrow and I'll put the subs on alert too. I have had a few of the lads on the phone to volunteer for early shifts, so we'll be fine. I will call you later.'

'Right-o boss,' said Wellings, before he read the list to his news editor who transcribed it in the fluent, speedy, flawless Teeline that was the envy of his newsroom. After Wellings hung up, Levitt went to his dining room table and started to draw up the death-knock rota for the morning. Unlike national newspapers there was no need for Levitt's journalists to barge into the fishing community's grief. Firstly, because there was no paper until the twenty-eighth, but more importantly there was a long-established routine between the local paper and the fishing folk when it came to tragedy.

There was none of the heartless foot-in-the-door insensitivity common with the nationals. Bereaved families always had ready photographs and other memorabilia – report cards, sports certificates and the like – belonging to their loved one to give to the "mister from the Mail." It was established practice. There was respect from the paper and indeed those bereaved expected the "mister from the Mail" to be the writer of what would probably be the only full tribute to mark the life of the perished soul.[5]

After a few phone calls Levitt had his team to visit the bereaved. The remainder of the night was spent drafting and redrafting his strategy.

He would be in his captain's chair at the centre of the hubbub of the newsroom in fewer than ten hours.

Richard Taylor's house, Boxing Day evening.

This time the authoritative *rat-tat-tat* on the front door was instantly recognised. Richard Taylor knew it was Mr Mac-Millan, as did his distressed daughter. The past few hours had been a silent ordeal for her. Jill had been unable to stop the reel of pictures that played in her tortured mind. She wondered if Tony had got the telegram telling him about the baby. Then she wondered if he was alive or dead, burned or drowned.

Minute after minute, hour after hour, Jill's mind raced. She went from hope to despair and back for every minute that passed since the previous visit. Those few hours flashed by for the clergyman, determined to put the poor young woman out of her torment as quickly as possible.

For the Taylors, the time since the vicar previously called was a slow, long, anxious waking nightmare. Richard Taylor's first thought was to protect her as best he could. When he rose to answer the door, he instructed his wife to keep Jill and the baby in the lounge.

The second that the door opened, Richard Taylor knew it was bad news. MacMillan's expression told him. Richard felt it was his role to hear that news, even though it was his daughter's bad news. But like most Hessle Road men of his generation, he did not see it that way. In his eyes, he was protecting his girl.

He braced himself as the Man from the Mission did his job. Richard stilled his nerves. In the living room his terrified girl strained to eavesdrop, although deep down she did not want to hear. In an instant, her heart was broken with three of the overheard words, *'missing, presumed dead'*.

MacMillan, in common with the neighbours, heard the poor young widow's *crie de coeur* echo as he reached his car.[6]

CHAPTER TWELVE

December 27, Newfoundland coast.

The towline repairs on Boxing Day added hours to Wool-dridge's mission to drag the blazing trawler to shore. It was about nine in the morning when the line snapped and early evening when repairs had finished and the exhausted skipper got under way again.

Throughout that night and into the morning he had a watch kept that reported to him on the status of the *St Finbarr*, which had her bow part-submerged. The stern-first tow was slow but so far effective. Wooldridge noted that the intense heat aboard the stricken vessel had expanded some of her plates and let more water in. This slowed her further, making her heavier and more difficult to control. Wooldridge realised the *St Finbarr* could go under at any minute, therefore a slow and steady tow was paramount for her successful recovery – and for the return to Hull of the men who had perished.

With luck, and the right amount of care, he thought he should be able to get her back. It meant more storm-tossed hours at four knots with a 1,139-ton albatross around his neck. Luck was in short supply for the *Orsino*'s commander but he was in the final stretch, with fewer than a hundred miles to St John's, and quietly confident.

Daylight came mid-morning on the twenty-seventh and Wooldridge was happy with reports from the watchmen that the *St Finbarr* was still steady. Her submerged bow had not gone much further under and four knots was still made. Wooldridge left the wheelhouse from time to time to reassure himself of his chances of getting the unlucky trawler to port. The two deckhands armed with axes, who guarded the warps, ready at a moment's notice to slice through them, were also an extra two pairs of eyes for the skipper.

By late afternoon the effort of towing the *St Finbarr* became steadily tougher. Her bow was now fully submerged. The ship looked as if she could go under bow-first at any minute. Wooldridge's constant watch told him that the *St Finbarr* was filling with sea with each hour passed. Expansion of the plates let in more water than first feared. Engine room reports said the stricken ship was heavier, slower and had become more dangerous. Wooldridge decided to continue and ordered the men at the warps to let the lines out so the part-submerged trawler would not pull harder on the *Orsino*.

The fact he had covered the distance that he had was a remarkable feat of seamanship and skill. Stern-towing is notoriously difficult in calm conditions but these two ships had not only fought together through winds of forty-five miles an hour and waves of more than thirty-five feet, but also battled driving snow and freezing rain. In the past forty-eight hours, the vessels travelled more than 200 miles and had made an emergency towline repair – and all this was done with the blazing ship's bow part-submerged.

About seven that evening, third engineer Dusty Miller was sent on deck to check on the men at the warps and report back.

Everyone aboard felt a gigantic jolt, followed by the collective shouting from the men on deck.

'She's going! Look!'

The *St Finbarr*'s stern lifted and pulled on the warps. The men with the axes awaited instruction. It was obvious she was sinking. Dozens of men, including some of the *St Finbarr* crew, watched.

Bosun Patrick was on deck to pass Wooldridge's orders to the men at the warp lines.

'The boss says don't cut the warps. Let them out as she goes to the bottom. Feed the warps out, lads. Follow her down. When she's settled, we'll retrieve the lines.'

The men at the warps started to loosen them as the pull of the *St Finbarr*'s descent became stronger. Her stern rose but her bow, although further down, seemed to stop sinking for a few seconds. In the wheelhouse Wooldridge noticed briefly that the *St Finbarr* had steadied. But any hope he had of resuming the tow was dashed in seconds. She was sinking. These were her death throes. Wooldridge telegraphed commands to the engine room to relent. On deck the warp men continued to loosen the lines that followed the *St Finbarr* as she rose stern first.

Third engineer Dusty Miller was stunned by what he saw next. He heard the collective gasps from the men at the rails and saw the *St Finbarr* was vertical, stern-up – and the slack tow lines hung from her. The men on the warps let the lines run free.

As he watched, Miller could not get out of his mind how what unfolded looked like the famous scene from the old movie *A Night to Remember*, when the *Titanic* rose and slid under the waves in seconds.

Dusty and the men watched as the *St Finbarr* went ninety-degrees, briefly vertical, her bow now completely below the water. Seconds later, she slipped under the waves. Her stern disappeared and the towlines followed her for 105 fathoms until she came to rest.

The perfect trawler became an impromptu grave, like thousands before her.

Her fight was over.

Waters frothed in a huge circle as wide as the ship that the Grand Banks had just claimed. A mass of bubbling sea reverted as quickly as it appeared. Gales whipped the wild waters and the now-still *Orsino* waited for the bump that would pull on her as the *St Finbarr* hit rock bottom. On deck, the men at warps had their work done for them.

A sudden jolt and movement told them that somewhere between there and the sea bed the lines had snapped.

Bosun Patrick and his team wound the warps back in. It took about fifteen minutes to wind in the lines and measure them as they so did.

'Look, we've got more back than we put out,' said one deckhand, 'How can that be?' Bosun Patrick answered, 'The tow line team must have done that repair well. We've been towing with our warp attached to the *Finbarr*'s. So, it must have been her line that snapped further down.'

In the wheelhouse Wooldridge made strides towards the wireless room. Sparks Bill Dunn was ready. The skipper dictated the telegram:

> 'FROM MASTER ORSINO – REGRET ST FINBARR SANK AT 1925 GMT 27TH. POSITION 51 48 05 N. 55 10 00 W. 105 FATHOMS. WEATHER NORTH 8 – SIGNED, WOOLDRIDGE.'1

That telegram disappeared into a mass of radio traffic and did not appear at the UK radio post at Portishead until hours later that night, before it was transferred on to the owners in the early hours of December 28.

Wooldridge continued toward St John's. His speed was now up to 12 knots and – as though the sea gods had played a joke – the weather began to improve. Wooldridge was unlucky indeed not to have landed his charge. His luck, which had been pushed for the past forty-eight hours, just ran out.

The remaining forty miles to St John's was going to be a cakewalk by comparison.

December 28, Hull

The mass anxiety that spread from Hessle Road across the great port city was finally soothed somewhat. Rumours soon were quashed and the living and the dead were identified.

Charles Levitt's news team had done its job well. That day's *Hull Daily Mail* also showed just how good David Mac-Millan and his team had been with theirs across Christmas and Boxing Day. On the twenty-seventh, Levitt's team followed in MacMillan's footsteps and picked up their tributes to the lost.

Fishing families knew the routine.

In a story headed *24 hours of agony for crew's families (Black-out delays news)* the paper recounted how families were left in the dark, not knowing if their loved ones were dead or alive. Readers learned how David MacMillan, Claude Weissenborn and their team had worked tirelessly to comfort families and told them what little they knew. The story described how news of the disaster had 'shattered gay Christmas night parties in the homes of the *St Finbarr*'s crew' and went on:

'[…] with the crew's homes a far apart as Hessle and Ganstead it was 2am before they were all contacted. Then news of the 13 survivors reached Hull and […] Mr MacMillan set out again until 5am, telling relatives.

All Boxing Day conflicting stories came in about the fate of the 12 remaining men.

Atmospheric conditions made contact with the two rescue trawlers almost impossible and the air was cluttered with ships' Christmas messages.

THE LAST CALL

Telephone links with Labrador were also overloaded and there was a two-and-a-half-hour delay even on emergency calls.

Throughout Boxing Day hope remained that the missing men were aboard the Sir Fred Parkes, which had been out of contact since the drama begun.

But by the evening it was confirmed that she had picked up no-one and soon afterwards news came that there were no survivors on board.

At 8pm on Boxing Day the welfare workers set out again to call on the homes of the 12 dead men. It was 3am yesterday (Tuesday, December 27) before the last was contacted.

(Hull Daily Mail, December 28, 1966)

Levitt's reporters and photographers produced reams of copy and ensured the newspaper's 133,000 copies sold out. Within half an hour there was not a copy left unsold across Hull. Head-and-shoulders photos of the twelve men who died were lined across the top of the broadsheet's front page. There were a few paragraphs on each of the perished, apart from sparehand John Matthews, of Liverpool Street, Hull, whose family were too distressed to talk. The front-page splash was headlined, **SURVIVORS LAND TONIGHT**, and outlined the tragic details – and the heroic rescue efforts of the *Orsino* which was headed to St John's. Inside, the human devastation of the Grand Banks disaster hit home.

EIGHTEEN IN THREE FAMILIES LOSE A FATHER – these seven words headed the heartrending vignettes that told of the tragedy visited on the bereaved:

'One of those killed – fish room chargehand John Smith, of 7 Ellingham Close, Longhill Estate, Hull – was only a fortnight ago awarded a Royal Humane Society certificate for his part in rescuing a shipmate off Flamborough Head last July. He had been going to sea since he was 14, but it was his first trip in an all-freeze trawler. He leaves three grown-up children.

Sparehand James Calvin Hamilton, 41, of 35 Eton Street, Hessle Road, leaves five daughters aged 12 to 21 and sons aged three to six. His wife Irene received a telegram from him, and his daughters Denise and Margaret had each been expecting an extra Christmas watch, when their father landed.

Six children are left behind by sparehand J. O'Dell, of 35 Uxbridge Grove, Hull. Their ages range from two to 11. Mr O'Dell had been at sea for 20 of his 34 years, mostly on conventional trawlers. Two of his brothers are at sea.

Another big family bereaved is that of the *St Finbarr*'s greaser Mr Harry Walter Smith, 52, of 11 Finchley Close, Ings Road, Hull. He leaves a widow, Ivy Louise Smith, and five sons and daughters, aged six to 21. Mr Smith ran away to sea when he was an eleven-year-old schoolboy at Chiltern Street School, Hull, and he had been with the *St Finbarr* for two years.

His eldest daughter, Mrs June Ann Jorgensen, 21, is married to a Merchant Navy officer, who is third mate in the *Custodian*.

Mr Smith's other sons and daughters are George Ronald William, 19, Kathleen Denise, 14, and Colin, six.

The death of deckie-learner David Young brought bereavement for the second time in three months to his home at 534 Inglemire Lane, Hull. Today, his deeply shocked mother was under sedation. In October, his father, Mr Thomas William Young, died after heart trouble forced him to leave the sea. Seventeen-year-old David had been a fisherman since he left Endike High School and had served in the *Primella* before joining the *St Finbarr*. His brother John was also a trawlerman until a back injury forced him to stay ashore.

Sparehand Stanley Brigham, 50, of 77 Shannon Road, Longhill Estate, was making only his second trip in the *St Finbarr*. He had been going to sea since he was 14. His son, Stanley, 26, is a sparehand in the Hull trawler *Arctic Hunter*. Mr Brigham also leaves a widow and a daughter, Mrs Maureen Linnell.

Christmas brought widowhood for the second time to Mrs Zena Sigurdsson, of 354 St George's Road, Hull. She lost her husband, sparehand Johann Sigurdsson, a 51-year-old Icelander. Her first husband died at sea when she was only 22.

Arthur* Harrison, of 4 Holly Villas, Flinton Street, Hull, a 20-year-old sparehand, had not been married very long, and leaves a baby daughter. It was his second trip aboard the *St Finbarr*.

Radio officer Thomas Gray, 48, of 31 Penshurst Road, Hessle, was making his first trip on the ill-fated trawler. He had served more than 15 years in Hull trawlers and was in the *Somerset Maugham* last year when she won the

---

* The *Hull Daily Mail* got Tony Harrison's name wrong and corrected it for the next edition with an apology.

Silver Cod Trophy for the year's record catch by a British trawler. Mr Gray, who leaves a widow, two married daughters and a son, worked in trawlers of the Newington Steam Trawling Co Ltd for many years.

Sparehand Robert Coulman, 19, is the eldest son of Mr and Mrs H Coulman of 32 Haddon Street, Hull. He went to sea when he was 15, and this was his third trip in the *St Finbarr*.

Sparehand Kenneth Pullen, 20, was the eldest son of Mr and Mrs James Pullen and had been going to sea for five years. He is the eldest of five children and his father was 25 years at sea. The present trip was his seventh in the *St Finbarr*, but this was the first time he had been away from home at Christmas.

Just before publication that morning Bob Wellings learned of another few rumours that he quashed on page one. One was that it was the *St Finbarr*'s engine room that had exploded. Another followed talk around the docks that somehow the two men lost in the rescue effort were killed because they had fallen from a breeches buoy/bosun's chair contraption that had snapped and sent them to their deaths. To be fair, some of the national papers had hinted at this too (with some of their interviews done from offices in New York via ship-to-shore calls without setting foot in Newfoundland. After all, why travel to the wilds if you don't need to?). In that day's *Hull Daily Mail*, Rear Admiral J A Ievers, manager of the Hull Steam Trawlers' Mutual Insurance and Protecting Co, told Wellings, 'It's pure imagination, these reports that there had been an engine room explosion aboard the *St Finbarr* and that survivors escaped by breeches buoy.

'We have no details at all yet. I would doubt if the men were rescued by breeches buoy, it is more likely they took to an inflatable life raft. And I do not think we shall know how the fire started until the survivors have been interviewed.' A third rumour Wellings put to bed was that more men had been picked up from a raft in the north Atlantic. Wellings' contacts in Lloyd's of London and the Ministry of Transport dismissed this as nonsense.

The city was no longer in the dark, but the cause of the explosion that killed the twelve men of *St Finbarr* remained a mystery.

December 28, the quayside at St John's, Newfoundland: 2300hours

A crowd watched as men hobbled down the side of the *Orsino* to the quay on the wood-and-rope ladder that forty-eight hours ago had been their precarious lifeline. The Hull trawler was the biggest on the fish dock that night and was easy to spot for Jack Fitzgerald, from St John's paper *The Daily News*. The crowd saw to the fore of the ship a scorched life raft bearing the name, *St Finbarr*.

Fitzgerald managed to grab a chat with one of the men who seemed to be counting the other men who gathered at the foot of the ladder on the quayside.

'Can I have your name, sir?' Fitzgerald said.

'It's Sawyer… Thomas Sawyer. I am the *St Finbarr* skipper.' Fitzgerald had guessed as much. The man in the suede shoes and moleskin trousers just had that air of authority about him. The little bell in the back of his head set off his "news sense" alarm. Bingo! Got the captain first time. Fitzgerald knew he had to make the most of the next few minutes as Sawyer looked impatient.

In sudden, potentially brief, interviews where the reporter must get his story, the practice is to keep questions short and to the point, and to keep them talking, no matter what.

'What happened, sir?'

'As I picked up the phone to put out a distress signal, I remember thinking she's blown up and the next thing I knew I was lying outside on the bridge on a funnel case with part of the telephone in my hand.'

'Wow! That's the intro!' thought the young reporter. He contained his excitement and continued his short bursts of interrogation whenever Sawyer paused for breath.

'Keep the questions coming,' the reporter told himself as he went into journalistic autopilot. 'Age? Family? Experience?

'Thirty-nine… married with four children… I've been a skipper for 12 years…'

And, most importantly… 'What happened next?'

Sawyer went on, 'Alerted by the warning, I went to investigate, but was driven back (by the smoke). It was very confusing, and it was impossible to identify other crew members. Some were naked, some half-clothed. I put out a distress signal that was picked up by the *Orsino*, which was about two miles away, I think.'

Sawyer went on to describe how he urged the men not to panic and put the ship on a circular course to 'enable the wind to blow the smoke from the deck'.

'What happened next?'

'It was during the time I was making the second distress call that the explosion blew me across the funnel case with the telephone still in my hand. All this happened in about seven minutes.'

He told how he and his two officers stayed aboard while the *Orsino* rescue party set up the tow – and how eventually the atrocious cold drove the last three *St Finbarr* men from their ship.

'Keep him talking,' the reporter told himself.

'Are you insured, sir?' Sawyer replied, 'No insurance was carried on the cargo of fish we were carrying, and the crew won't get anything either!

'The owners have been good. Watson Hall, the owner's son, met the ship earlier and was very concerned for the men. It's a family firm and we are treated like a family.'

Sawyer saw his men were gathered and there were taxis waiting alongside. Fitzgerald realised his interview would end soon.

'What was it like out there, captain?'

'The seas were very rough and it was very cold. When the *Sir Frederick Parkes* arrived, they tried to fire a line aboard but we couldn't do it. It was ten degrees below zero and high seas, and the conditions were very bleak.'

'What do you think forced the ship to sink from the tow?'

'Intense heat and rough seas must have pulled the seams of the boat apart, causing her to sink.' With that the skipper went back to his men.

A passing *Orsino* crewman was next to be grabbed by Fitzgerald but that exchange was very brief. 'What happened, sir?' The crewman looked at the reporter as if he was daft, and said, 'I don't know. Nobody knows, it's a big mystery.' The man joined the crowd.

Men near the ship and on the quayside seemed to freeze as the *Orsino*'s pulleys swung a load overhead. It was wrapped in a Union Jack, which in turn had a heavy woollen blanket wrapped around it, leaving only parts of the flag showing.

'Hats off, lads,' said one of the deckhands.

Bystanders, crew and survivors stood still, and some blessed themselves as the body of Curly Smith was lowered to the ambulance that took him to his temporary rest at the local morgue.[2] As Curly's ambulance left, it was followed by a second containing the *St Finbarr*'s first mate Walt Collier, whose ulcer had burst. The quayside was quiet, and the crowd dispersed.

The taxis moved in convoy with the men from the *St Finbarr* inside. Fitzgerald knew where they were headed. There would be no more for him to do that night. His colleague Dave Butler would do the follow-ups in the morning at the hotel the survivors were booked into.

Fitzgerald went to find a phone box to put over the copy that would be the first front page lead after the Christmas holiday.

If he had followed them, he would have got an added human interest story, and maybe even some amusing pictures. The taxis peeled off from the dockside and headed for the town centre en route to their accommodation. Thick snow covered the empty pavements and lay heavy on the occasional car by the roadside as the dead-of-night cab convoy whished on the slushy roads, and passed clapperboard houses, silhouetted against the dark snow-cloud-filled skies. Houses, occasionally illuminated by passing headlamp beams, contained families unaware that the cars that briefly disturbed their sleep in the wee small hours carried some of the luckiest men ever to have visited St John's.

After twenty minutes or so, the taxi fleet stopped outside the ornate façade of the Bowring Brothers department store in Water Street. Its brightly lit frontage stood out among the other large, closed shops nearby.

Icy air hit the men as they shuffled from the cabs into the shiny department store.

A uniformed commissioner welcomed the partly clothed, partially frostbitten crewmen and they were ushered in like hobbling royalty. These fellas could not have looked more incongruous. Inside it got weirder. Each of the Hull trawlermen was met by an individually appointed salesman and on standby was a team draped with tape measures over waistcoats. An immaculately dressed chargehand appeared and told the men to choose any clothing they needed.

'The tailors will measure you should you need it, gentlemen, and the accounts will be sent to your employers.' The somewhat dazed trawlermen, led by the salesmen, wandered from rail to rail and shelf to shelf and picked out their new clothes.

'It's a bit of a step up from Waistell's or Manny Marx – "the fifty-bob tailor"[3] is this place lads, innit?!' one of the deckies quipped.

And for the first time in days the men laughed.

'And don't worry about the cost, gentlemen,' added the immaculate floorwalker.

'Don't worry mate, we won't,' came the not-so-stage-whispered reply from one of the crew.[4] The money-no-object instruction was genuine. After all, the Bowrings who owned the store also owned the shipping agents that acted for Hamlings of Hull. It was win-win for them. The men spent almost an hour being kitted out with new coats, suits, socks, shoes, underwear and hats under the supervision of their individually appointed personal shoppers.

Mr Floorwalker announced, 'Gentlemen, it's time to go to your hotel now,' in a sonorous voice that suggested he had spoken to a group of out-of-town businessmen rather a desperate huddle of rescued sailors. Sawyer led his men in a semblance of order to the huge doors that led out to the snowy streets. A brief burst of icy cold hit them as they clambered back to the warmth of the cars that set off for their accommodation.

The store staff set about the task of getting the purchases ready for their impromptu customers. A few hours later, dozens of neatly tied parcels waited in name-labelled Bowring Brothers bags and boxes at the Cochrane Hotel, in time for the men to be suitably attired for their stay at the grand old hotel as well as for their flight home.

The *Orsino*'s radio man Bill Dunn had agreed to talk to Jack Fitzgerald's colleague Dave Butler from the *St John's Daily News*. Dunn had a photo of the *St Finbarr* taken just minutes before it sank which he had promised the newsman. Not only that, the fisherman did not want anything in return, other than a promise of some prints from the developed film. The pair agreed to meet over breakfast in the galley of the *Orsino,* as the ship was due to return to the Grand Banks the following day (Friday). Dunn told Butler, 'We had only been in Labrador for twenty-four hours after making our maiden voyage from Hull. We did some fishing but were laying-to because of the bad weather. I was awakened by one of the deckhands who said I was wanted on the bridge. When I arrived there, I was told by the captain that we had received a Mayday (distress) signal on the VHF radio. I then went out to look and could see ahead of us a ship with her bridge on fire about five miles away. I went back to the wireless room and sent mayday signals to other ships in the area asking them to make a bearing with us.'

Dunn went on to tell how the *St Finbarr* was stopped dead in the water and radio communication was impossible so the crews shouted to each other.

'The sea was very rough and there was a strong wind. We could see some of the *St Finbarr*'s men at the stern of the ship and flames were shooting out of the bridge and the front half of her was covered with smoke,' he said.

The *Orsino* wireless man recounted the drama of the men's rescue and went on to tell how the skipper, mate and chief were forced to return on the *St Finbarr*'s lifeboat when the *Orsino* workboat went adrift.

The most poignant part of Dunn's report was when he recounted how the body of Curly Smith was recovered. He said, 'We received word from the German trawler *Hamburg* that they had picked up the body of one of the men who had fallen from the ladder. So, we had to drop a life raft over the side on a long line. The German ship came up behind, secured the body in the raft and we pulled it in.'[5]

Butler knew this was a great human interest story and first-rate eyewitness account. His editors agreed and decided to use it verbatim. They also decided to "by-line" the radio operator – in the style, '*by WE Dunn, as told to* **DAVE BUTLER News Staff Writer**.'

Butler and Fitzgerald's exclusive stories for *The Daily News* were picked up by the national news agency Canadian Press, followed by Associated Press and others. News telegrams and telexes flashed around the world and hundreds of "creeds" in hundreds of case rooms alerted thousands of journalists and millions of readers, listeners and viewers worldwide.

Bowring Brothers had done the men of *St Finbarr* proud. Parcels arrived in time for the crewmen to take to the grand dining table in the Cochrane Hotel.

Just seventy-two hours earlier they were as near to death as they would ever be. Most still suffered frostbite, burns, cuts and shock to varying degrees, but any observer would have been pushed to see anything other than a group of robust, smartly dressed men.

Jonathan Watson Hall, the young executive who had flown out on Christmas Day, joined his men at the table. He was pleased they were all properly dressed. Watson Hall had been looking out for all their needs since he arrived. His concern manifested itself in constant nervous checking of the crew. He was like a demented mother hen. Every five minutes there was a query. This had gone on since he had met the survivors at the quayside.

'Is there anything else you need? ... Are you sure everything is OK? ... Is there any more I can do?'

Watson Hall's fussing had not gone unnoticed by the men, who, when he was out of earshot, mockingly mimicked him in a faux-posh voice. Flights home had been arranged by the agents, Bowrings. All the men were booked on the 7am flight, except Walt Collier, the mate who was still recovering from the operation on his burst ulcer. Also, Taff Evans was still to give his evidence to the local Board of Trade inquiry. It was planned that he and Collier would fly back together.

To the sad surprise of the men, the body of Curly Smith would not be coming home either, even though Watson Hall had booked the old man's remains on to a plane the day previously.

'I want *all* of my men to come home together,' Watson Hall told the agents. But news from Curly's widow in Hull had been sent, telling them she wanted her man, who had run away to sea when he was just eleven years old, to be put to final rest on the Grand Banks.

The men of *St Finbarr* would have one more night of fading luxury in this famous hotel where, local lore had it, communist Leon Trotsky once stayed en route from New York to a Mother Russia in the throes of revolution.[6]

Next day in the foyer, taxi drivers waited to take the men to the airport. Skipper Sawyer gathered his crew in the hotel lounge bar and waited for Watson Hall to join them.

The tall, slim, bespectacled trawler boss wasted no time in getting across to the tables where his men sat. Almost immediately on arrival he asked, 'Everything all right, chaps? Is there anything I can do?'

The men laughed, and one of the deckhands quipped, 'Why don't you pop to the bar and get yourself a drink, Mr Hall. You're in a bloody worse state than us, sir!'

Friday, December 30, 1966 – the Hull Daily Mail newsroom.

Hull Daily Mail news editor Charles Levitt knew from the Press Association (PA) telexes and briefings from docks reporter Bob Wellings that the men of the *St Finbarr* would be home later that day. PA photos had been wired earlier from Prestwick Airport in Ayrshire, Scotland, showing the crewmen's return.

Hamlings had arranged for them to be driven back to Hull. Levitt knew he had a window from late afternoon onwards to get the survivors interviewed, photographed and copy filed for the next day ready for the sub-editors' desk to process. He expected fuller results from the survivors' families; after all, they had happy stories to tell and would be far easier to persuade. Levitt dispatched his reporters and photographers in pairs to doorstep the lucky families and bring back their personal stories.

On the sub-editors' desk, it was now as mad as it could get. A second disaster complete with "miracles" had happened closer to home that lunchtime. (This meant some subs worked flat-out on the breaking story while others concentrated on the latest from *St Finbarr*, alongside the masses of copy for the remainder of that day's newspaper.) The news from Newfoundland was demoted to the sidebar on page one when reports came in that a Hunter fighter jet from nearby RAF Leconfield had crashed into – and demolished – two cottages – one was the Old Rectory. No-one was badly hurt and the local vicar, Norman Dickinson, had a "miraculous escape" with just a broken arm when his home was reduced to rubble. The jet's pilot ejected safely and was picked up by a helicopter from the Search and Rescue Squadron. So, the tale earned its front-page status.

Sub-editors on the *St Finbarr* story put together a front-page side lead and background reports for page five, while Levitt and his county news editor Ian Stockdale pulled together the local disaster for page one. It was one hell of a news day. On one side of the horseshoe-shaped desk sub-editors swore and screeched and hollered for more copy and pictures of the jet crash as the deadline drew ever near.

On the other they measured page layouts, cast off headlines to fit and dropped in the *St Finbarr* stories and photos. A front-lead-sized space was left for the jet crash – with just ten minutes before the third edition's afternoon deadline. The subs raged as subs do, while Levitt and Stockdale – two of the most unflappable men in the building, if not in the industry – managed to get their jet crash copy polished and ready to go with minutes to spare. Levitt had a sound reputation for quick work under pressure, but he could lose his temper as deadlines drew close and if reporters did not type fast enough. Stockdale, however, a gentle, churchgoing, cricket-mad, even-tempered man, with an unfathomable reserve of calm, was a steadier hand. No-one had ever even heard him swear. He just got on with the job, no matter how busy – and it had rarely been busier than that day. Together they worked well together.

Completed copy, pictures and layouts were put in eighteen-inch-long plastic cylinders, six inches in circumference, and placed into the huge vacuum pipes that fired them overhead, across the newsroom ceiling and into the case room, where they dropped. (It was a system not unlike those used in old-fashioned department stores to send orders to stock rooms.) The newsroom buzz was at its peak with minutes to go. The deadline would be met. The final cylinder was fired when the case room manager appeared at the news desk. The pink PA RUSH telex paper in his hand matched the colour of his sweaty face. He gave the telex over to Stockdale.

'Fuck,' said the harassed county news editor as his stunned colleagues fell silent. Levitt took the news brief from him.

It read: 'ORSINO IN HARBOUR COLLISION'.

A second glance by Levitt immediately put the newsroom and Stockdale's mind at ease. The intro read: 'The Hull trawler *Orsino*, which rescued 13 survivors from the *St Finbarr*, was in collision with a cargo ship in St John's Newfoundland last night.'

Levitt did not have to read further, He handed the story to a sub-editor with the instruction, 'There's no real damage or death, so just five pars, page one.' He turned to Stockdale and added, 'That got you going, didn't it, Ian!'

While the newsroom fed the case room for one more edition, Levitt's pairs of newsmen were out across the city and county tracking down families of the *St Finbarr*'s survivors to bring copy and pictures in time for the next day's paper, the production of which would start as that day's coverage ended. That was the routine on this huge city and county paper that sold almost 140,000 copies daily from Monday to Saturday across four editions.

Hornsea, East Yorkshire.

Set back from the main Rolston Road in the small seaside town of Hornsea, East Yorkshire, was St Alcuin, the detached home of Skipper Tom Sawyer. The posh house was named after Sawyer's first command with Hamlings.

In the living room, a photographer set up a shot. The immaculately dressed trawler commander, in shirt sleeves but wearing a dark tie, posed surrounded by wife, Hilda, their three daughters, Marilyn, seventeen, Veronica, fifteen, and Janet, thirteen. Nine-year-old son Steven sat on his father's knee. The snapper captured perfectly the brave man surrounded by his loving family. Anyone who saw this picture would be incredulous if they knew that only a few days earlier this courageous skipper had come within an ace of losing his own life as he stayed aboard his doomed command with two senior officers to ensure the escape of what was left of his crew. Sawyer spoke freely to the reporter in his impressive, calm manner.

'I cannot praise the crew of the *Orsino* enough. They showed wonderful seamanship in their attempts to save the crew of the *St Finbarr*. I should like to express my deepest sympathy with the families of those who were lost. It was not a crew aboard the *St Finbarr* – it was a family. We were all together. It was a happy ship.

'I have never worked with a crew like it. I shall return to the sea when I feel better but I have no plans at present. I shall slip away when the inquiry is finished. It starts in Hull on Monday and I will be there to give initial evidence with the others.'[7]

At bosun Eric Samms' house in Shannon Road, Hull, the men from the local paper were turned away sharply but politely. Newfie Samms, a six-feet-plus bearded man-mountain, said in his Canadian drawl, 'Sorry, boys, I don't wanna talk. Maybe another time, eh?' The two newsmen left as asked. Halfway down the path one quipped, 'I wouldn't want to be the foot-in-the-door merchant from the nationals who gets on his wrong side!'

It was a better reception for Levitt's men at the home of Newfie Samms' shipmate and friend, chief engineer Hughie Williams. Hughie had his feet up and was opening the presents his family had saved for him when the *Hull Daily Mail* duo arrived. Williams looked like any dad at Christmas in his favourite armchair surrounded by his wife and kids. But Williams' demeanour and appearance were deceptive.

His feet were up because the frostbite had made it difficult for him to stand for any length of time. The brave engineer explained how he tried in vain to save more of his shipmates.

'I tried to get back below into the engine room, where I knew there were men that needed help. But I was driven back,' Williams said.

He went on to explain why he stayed with the skipper and the mate while the men were placed in the life raft and sent towards the rescue vessel *Orsino*. 'We thought we could still save the ship – and we could have if weather conditions had been reasonable. It was the cold that beat us, not the sea.

'When I got home, I just broke down and sobbed like a child. These men that died were not just shipmates. They were my pals as well.'

The reporter asked if Hughie would return to sea. He replied, 'I am hoping to take up one of the new freezer ships. After all, I've got to live.' In the next day's newspaper, there was an added paragraph that read, *'His wife, Mary, mother of four, spoke of the agonising waiting.'* It was the first time since Christmas that Mary Williams had spoken at all for days. She had been struck dumb and took to her bed, after she heard the BBC bulletin that announced that her husband's ship was on fire and casualties were unknown.

Her parents, who had visited from London, took over, and in a great pretence of normality, told the kids that their mam was unwell and had taken to her bed. The kids carried on with Christmas with their grandparents keeping up the charade. Even when the official news came that Hughie was safe, Mary refused to believe it until she saw her man for herself.[8]

There was a Christmas cake on the dining room table at second engineer George Grinlaw's house in Cardigan Road. In the kitchen, the chicken that his wife had bought specially was to be the centrepiece for that day's belated festive feast. His kids, Gary, nine, Kevin, five, Lorraine, four, and baby Aileen, just nine months, prepared for the party George's twenty-nine-year-old wife Brenda had promised them.

She told the newsmen, 'I told the kids we would have a proper Christmas when their dad got home and that's what we are going to do!' George took the reporter to one side and added, 'The first thing I did when I got back was to go and see Taff Evans' wife to her know he is OK and will be home after he gives his evidence to the local inquiry.' Grinlaw also praised ever-anxious trawler boss, Jonathan Watson Hall. George said, 'Mr Hall really looked after the crew. He bought us anything we wanted and paid for telephone calls to the wives for the men.'

Eric Petrini, the twenty-one-year-old deckhand badly burned when he had to lay down his best friend in the fires below the *St Finbarr*'s decks, said little when visited at his house, off St George's Road. He was still in shock.

Eric's dad Harold said, 'I am sorry for anyone who has lost a relative on board that ship, but I am thankful to God from the bottom of my heart that He sent my son back.'

Eric added, 'It was marvellous organisation by the *St Finbarr*'s four officers and the skipper and the crew of the *Orsino*.'

Another second engineer, thirty-year-old Trevor Hardwick, of Woodcock Street, off Hessle Road, also praised the *Orsino* men. In the living room of his tidy little terrace house, surrounded by his twenty-nine-year-old wife Shirley and his kids, Susan, ten, Stephen, four, and Tony, two, the rescued fisherman said, 'When we got on board the *Orsino* the crew let us have their bunks and clothing. The rescue organisation was excellent too.'

When asked if he would return to sea, Trevor added, 'I don't think this will stop me. But for now, I am just happy to be home safe.'

St Finbarr's greaser John Scott, the first man to be put on the life raft, was back at the sparse room at the Queen Mary Hostel at Goulton Street's Royal Mission to Deep Sea Fishermen by mid-afternoon, but was unable to stay indoors and longed for the solace of the pub. When newsmen turned up they were told he was out.

'He's got the right idea – probably down the boozers. It'd be nice if we had the time to search a few of them for him, eh?!' quipped the photographer as the pair went on to find the next name and address on the list Charles Levitt gave them six hours earlier.

In the Strickland Arms, one of the many pubs off Hessle Road, a busy, bustling bar was rendered silent by an immaculately turned-out man in a radio operator's uniform, who shouted, 'I want to buy everyone in this pub a drink! Now!'

The building burble of drink orders replaced the short-lived silence.

The radio man took his large glass of rum in hand and shouted again. 'Raise your glasses and drink with me… all of you. I've lost a great friend.'

A semblance of silence returned, and the man continued, 'Drink to Tommy Gray!' Seconds after the toast, he left as quickly as he had arrived. Sitting unnoticed in the corner alone, drunk greaser John Scott raised a glass again for the man he had seen fall to his death just days earlier.

In Portobello Street, two men arguing under the street-lamp drew attention to themselves. Curtains twitched. It was Friday night after closing time.

'There's nothing in it, mate. You're dragging me back here for bugger all. He's not back yet. Probably in the boozers, if he's got any sense… like we should be by now,' said the tall, thin, balding man with a shock of mad-professor style hair. He had a large camera around his neck. His Nosferatu-esque silhouette cast long across the pavement under the sodium beam, which caught in shadow the curls of smoke from one of his omnipresent cigs.

'C'mon, one more go, Reg,' said the young reporter, who was as keen as Reg was experienced. The older man knew the kid reporter, whose name he could not remember, was right, but he had not had a drink all day and it was dangerously near closing time.

'Right then, kid, one more go, then that's it. Levitt told me the rest of them have filed their copy. Let's get this over with before we find ourselves without the chance of a pint!'

'Cheers, Reg, you're a pal,' said the younger man.

'Yeah, a regular fucking saint, kid!' Reg drawled in his East Midlands accent. Reg Lucy – whose chain-smoking and drinking exploits were as legendary as his incredible newsgathering talent – called everybody kid or duck, dependent on gender, especially those whose names he had not learned yet. The pair walked a further ten yards when they heard a piercing scream. 'What the f…'

The young reporter found himself running behind a reanimated Reg. His camera pointed at the source of the scream. A middle-aged housewife had run towards a heavy-set, smartly dressed fellow in his late forties as he left a taxi. The man dropped a couple of carrier bags and enveloped the woman in a bear hug. The reporter glanced at the last name on his list and thought, 'Looks like we've found Harry at last!' The newsmen had been around to the *St Finbarr* cook Harry Prince's house earlier but there was no-one at home… or at least no-one had answered the door.

The vindicated newsman whipped his pencil and notebook from his coat pocket in time to hear the woman blurt, 'Oh, God! I can't believe it! You're home!' The housewife ran down the garden path that led to the neat little semi-detached set back from the road.

'Let me pay the cabbie, love,' said the man as his wife clung to him, but she would not let him go. He managed to free one arm and reach into his pocket and pull out a ten-bob note, which he thrust toward the rolled-down window on the driver's side.

'Keep the change, mate,' said Harry, still in his Dora's vice-like hug.

'Cheers, our kid!' The cabbie drove off with his hundred per cent tip. Dora dragged Harry up the path. Her arm was now wrapped around his waist. The newsmen followed them. As the pair disappeared into the house, Reg said loudly, '*Hull Daily Mail*, Mr Prince. Can we have a brief word, please?'

'Aye, of course. You might as well come in seeing as how you're over the doorstep!'

Once inside the couple talked and talked. It was a reporter's dream interview. Harry slumped on to the sofa and Dora was still with him.

Her arms were now around his neck as she spoke. Their pedigree Sealyham dog – Chanta Cherie Finbarr (named after her master's trawler, but called Cherie for short!) – leapt into the fray too.

'I just can't believe it,' Dora said. 'It's the second time Harry's survived a wreck.'

The reporter could not believe his luck. What a story! He fired off questions as the snapper fired off shots. Harry told how he had survived the *St Celestin* sinking, off Bear Island in 1958 after the infamous collision with the *Arctic Viking*. The notebook filled with details of the past survival. Back then, all hands were saved, unlike now, of course, when only thirteen from twenty-five had survived.

Before Harry continued, Reg managed to get him and Dora to pose with their dog for a great photo that he knew would be used large next day. With the sure shot taken, Reg let Harry go on to tell about his escape from the *St Finbarr*. (The snapper even put in a few questions himself to help his young colleague along. What Reg did not know about door-stepping was not worth knowing.)

On his escape from the *St Finbarr*, Harry said, 'I was leaving the galley when the ship started to blaze. If I had turned in, I would not be here now. At seven-thirty there was nothing. At twenty-five to eight, the ship was ablaze. That's how quick the fire went through her. I managed to get off in the raft with nine others while the skipper, chief and mate stayed aboard. There was no panic. It was very well organised and the lads behaved very well. I have nothing but high praise for the skipper, the mate and the chief engineer for the hard work they did in getting us off the ship. I don't know if I will return to the sea, after all they say things happen in threes, eh?'

'Words just cannot describe how I feel,' said Dora, and found what words she could. 'I am a lucky wife...very lucky indeed.'

'I still don't know whether this is a dream or not after what we have been through,' Harry added. 'We are the luckiest thirteen men in the world.'

CHAPTER THIRTEEN

Monday, September 19, 1967, Board of Trade Inquiry, The Guild-hall, Hull, 9.30am.

The lawyers, trawlermen, widows and fatherless children were dwarfed by the black, ornate wrought-iron gates that were pushed open by uniformed court ushers.

The crowd drifted along the oak-panelled corridor towards Court Number Three, the biggest in the Guildhall – home to the city's law courts and civic offices.

A small poster pinned under of one of the opaque glass portholes on one of the heavy oak double doors of the courtroom read: 'For the formal investigation listed as Case No. S478, into the sinking of m.f.v (motor fishing vessel) *St Finbarr.*'

This courtroom was normally reserved for the Hull stipendiary magistrate. On this day, it hosted the Wreck Commissioner, Judge Peter Bucknill QC.

It was midway down an oak-panelled spinal corridor out from which sprung offices and consulting rooms (for lawyers and clients) on one side and the six magistrates' courts on the other.

At the east end a crosswise passage and stairwell led to a square reception from which a double staircase rose to the council committee rooms, main civic chamber and grand banqueting hall.

Its exterior would not look out of place in Whitehall. (It is often used as a "movie double" for that area to this day.) The interior of panelled corridors, marble staircases, domed skylights and Renaissance revival-style murals made it every inch the civic temple to commerce favoured by Victorian city fathers of the industrial powerhouses of the north. However, it was very much a twentieth-century building, eight years in the construction and completed in 1914. Only the clock outside above the eastern entrance remained from the old town hall it replaced. The Guildhall was designed by the English architect Sir Edwin Cooper, whose portfolio also included the Royal Star and Garter injured servicemen's home in London.[1]

There was a constant clatter on the granite floor as the corridor filled with nervous defendants, busy lawyers and police officers checking the notes to which they would later ask the beak to refer. Directly outside Court Three was a calmer affair. Dr Lionel Rosen spoke quietly with families of the lost men that he represented. Further along, Skipper Tommy Sawyer spoke with his brief, HM Loncaster. In one of the consulting rooms opposite, Barry Sheen QC, a top London barrister, and his junior counsel Nigel Phillips, hired by local maritime specialist solicitors Andrew M Jackson and Co, spoke with clients

Jonathan Watson Hall and his father Michael, of Thomas Hamlings and Co, owners of the *St Finbarr*.

Inside Court Three, Judge Peter Bucknill QC sat in the centre of the judges' bench, which was some seven feet above the rest of courtroom. Above him was the royal coat of arms and the three-crown crest of the city and county of Kingston upon Hull. To Bucknill's left were Captain RG Freeman and Commander FM Paskins, and on the right Dr EG Corbett.

These men were appointed by the Board of Trade to assist the judge. Below them in the area usually reserved for the prosecution were solicitors Richard Stone and George Beattie, up from London to represent the Board of Trade.

There were also two Liverpool-based lawyers for the electrical firm Campbell and Isherwood, which wired the *St Finbarr*. A further pair of lawyers from Hull were there on a watching brief of the Port Glasgow-based shipbuilders Ferguson Brothers.

Masses of evidence had been gathered, affidavits taken and initial witness statements submitted along with technical reports. It was expected it would take ten days to hear all the evidence.[2] The first batches came from the local hearing held in Newfoundland directly after the tragedy. The initial Hull-based court hearing was opened and adjourned in January 1967 as some of the *St Finbarr* men were still deemed too ill to attend. The Board of Trade spent months pulling together all the information for this hearing. Half an hour before the inquiry was reconvened, Rosen spoke with the women he represented and then went to a consulting room where he perused his papers and notes. He composed himself for the case ahead. His last-minute revision was force of habit, but he had committed most of his brief to memory.

This doyen of maritime lawyers had a reputation across England for fierce and forensic cross-examination.

Dr Lionel Rosen was a polymath. His gained his first law degree aged just nineteen by external examination from the London University, having studied at the Hull Technical College. His master's degree followed soon after and his doctorate was achieved before his twenty-fifth birthday, by which time he had become a partner – the Rosen in Pearlman and Rosen – a practice founded by Alderman Benno Pearlman, local Labour politician and former Lord Mayor of Hull.

As well his success in the law, Dr Rosen was a local public intellectual, a prominent member of the city's Literature and Philosophical Society, who gave regular lectures on literature and art. He had served as a captain in the Royal Army Ordnance Corps in the Second World War, and was also an expert in electrics, communications and logistics, (although Mrs Rosen would joke that at home he could not wire a plug!).

In common with the building where he conducted most of his practice, Dr Rosen's appearance was deceptive. In his winged, starched collar, silk tie, black three-piece pin-striped suit, complete with gold fob watch and chain, he looked every inch the conservative Victorian brief. He was approaching his sixtieth year, forty of which had been dedicated to the law. Rosen was a lifelong socialist, Labour city councillor and long-time legal advisor (often pro bono) for the Transport and General Workers' Union, which represented the trawlermen.

Widely experienced, he was considered one of the country's leading experts in maritime law.[3] He knew the drill all too well. With Board of Trade hearings, mountains of technical reports and affidavits were entered to evidence, backed by questioning of relevant witnesses. It was this aspect of the hearings where Rosen excelled. He had four main points in mind that he aimed to bring to the court's attention. The four men in his sights were the *St Finbarr*'s chief engineer; the previous radio operator, whose affidavit told of earlier fires aboard the doomed ship; the first mate, whose evidence showed glaring errors in fire drill practice; and the skipper, who Rosen intended to harry and bully into accepting some culpability for the loss of some of the twelve lives.

He wanted to show skipper Sawyer as being below-par in the face of danger and demonstrate that his order to abandon ship was premature.

The lawyer intended to build a picture of a ship that had unattended faults that led to a series of fires. Rosen prepared a case for poor health and safety on board ship, and a disastrous failure to fight the fatal fire that followed.

Inside Court Three, the bench immediately in front of the judge had a line of lawyers sitting behind bundles of papers and files, each of which rested on the long ledge in front. Behind was the dock – and to either side of that is where the public sat. The hum of their whispered conversations halted.

'All rise! Let all those today having anything to do with this hearing in Her Majesty's court, draw nearer and give their attention!'

That theatrically delivered announcement from the Clerk to the Court saw the crowded courtroom rise as one. They were seated seconds later after the lawyers, clerks and police bowed before the Bench. The court of inquiry into the fate of the *St Finbarr* had begun. The families sat in attentive silence... It was time for Board of Trade lawyer Richard Stone's opening statement.

'The fact that so many managed to escape from the fire aboard this vessel shows they were clearly very lucky to do so,' he began. 'The vessel and her gear had been well maintained by her owners. However, the fire spread with such rapidity and fierceness that it proved beyond the powers of those on board to control. It was a wholly unexpected fire. Every member of the crew below the rank of bosun was turned in or asleep – they had spent much of the preceding night attempting to fish.'

Stone explained that fishing was abandoned in the early hours and the skipper allowed the men to each have a drink of whisky and some beer to mark Christmas before they turned in and that it was intended to fish again the following day.

'On the evidence before the Board of Trade it is not suggested that drink could have played any part in the cause of the fire nor in the failure to contain it and the subsequent loss of life.'

He continued, 'On Christmas morning, it was freezing hard and the vessel was hove-to in a north-easterly gale, force eight, about one hundred miles from the coast of Labrador. At approximately 7.30am fire broke out on board and spread rapidly.

'The fire is thought to have originated in the vicinity of the greaser's cabin on the port side of the lower deck in the crew accommodation.

'Five minutes later, the third engineer on watch in the engine room saw smoke being drawn in by the main engine turbine blower and shortly afterwards observed smoke and flames coming through the lower-deck port-side entrance.

'Now, on the evidence available, the Board is not suggesting that the cause of the fire, or the inability to control, or the resulting loss of life was due to any wrongful act or default of any person.

'This inquiry has three main purposes and those are firstly to find out what happened and what was the story. Secondly, to determine if anybody was at fault – and what could be learnt from the facts for the future – so that the tragedy was not repeated.'

The lawyer told how a blast caused by a sudden expansion of hot air blew the doors and windows out of the wheelhouse and the skipper was thrown out on to the casing seconds after trying to make a further Mayday. However, the Hull stern trawler *Orsino* had already responded to his first distress call. Stone continued, 'Fire spread rapidly to the bridge and the skipper gave orders to prepare the lifeboat and inflatable life rafts. Two life rafts were launched on either side of the vessel but the starboard-side raft became detached and was lost.

'The other life rafts on board were destroyed by fire. About 9.30am twelve of the crew were drifted over to the *Orsino* in the remaining life raft, but two of them were lost while attempting to embark on to the *Orsino*. The skipper, mate and chief engineer remained on board and were transferred to the *Orsino* by 2.15pm.'

The court heard the chain of events of the disaster and how the *St Finbarr* was hitched to the *Orsino* at about 7.30pm that Christmas night, and how that stern-first tow parted the following morning at about 8am but was reconnected that evening.

'Two hundred and three miles later the *St Finbarr* foundered and sank, just thirty miles from safety,' Stone added. The cause of the devastating fire was unknown but he had evidence that would show it was caused by a catastrophic failure in the ship's electrics.[4]

Next day, Richard Stone's opening statement picked up on the same theme: 'Evidence gathered by experts for the Board of Trade suggests that the fire that destroyed the ship was due to an electrical fault.

'It was probable that the origin of the fire was in the crew accommodation on the lower deck near to the greasers' cabin. It appears the fire spread rapidly fore and aft in the accommodation. Our experts indicate that the origin of the fire was above the deckhead lining.

'Arcing in a light fixture due to a loose connection or weak spring to the bayonet connection with the bulb might have ignited insulation which could have set fire to softwood in the vicinity.' Stone went on to describe how such a short-circuit caused an overload which in turn melted the cables and let off an inflammable gas. The overload could have been sufficient to cause an inflammable gas in the circuit. When the fire reached the next cabin, it would have ready access to the deck above. The effect of having gas leaving a point in the cable was like a blow lamp.

'This would explain not only the rapid spread of the fire but also the smoke associated with it. It could also explain the expansions of hot air. Once the fire had reached a considerable intensity there were plastic-type materials which could be involved in the combustion.'[5]

Nervous, young shipping company executive Jonathan Watson Hall looked as incongruous in the dock of Court Three as he did in the wheelhouse of a trawler.

In a soft tone, almost as if to put him at ease, the Wreck Commissioner Judge Peter Bucknill addressed him. 'Mr Hall, I am concerned with how the fire happened and to take any recommendation which might avoid this sort of thing happening again.' Hall nodded acknowledgement to the Bench and readied himself to give his evidence.

Dr Lionel Rosen was not so comforting. 'Is it not the case that the *St Finbarr* was plagued by a series of electrical breakdowns and faults?' Before Hall could answer, Rosen went on, 'I have an affidavit from a former chief engineer, now resident in New Zealand, that described voyage after voyage on which there had been faults.'

Hall replied, 'All outstanding electrical faults had been dealt with by local contractors before the last voyage, under the command of Skipper Sawyer, a first-class man in whom I have every confidence.' Hall added that there had been delays before the final trip to ensure that the electrics and other issues were dealt with before sailing.

The Board of Trade brief Richard Stone cut in with, 'What sort of electrical problems did the *St Finbarr* suffer, Mr Hall?'

Hall had his answers. 'There were problems suffered on previous voyages, but they were the sort of electrical faults common on a vessel of that kind – and none of those reported were in the accommodation areas.'

But Rosen was not giving up.

'Mr Hall, because there were more electrical faults than usual, did this not give you personal concerns?'

'Yes, but in as far as the refrigeration machinery was concerned as I was worried that voyages could be curtailed because of it. In fact, some were.'

'Yes, and do you agree that you sent experts out to Newfoundland to deal with such issues on board?'

'Yes, I did,' said Hall.

Rosen continued, 'There were throughout the previous thirteen voyages of the *St Finbarr* a series of electrical breakdowns […] voyage after voyage in which there were faults.'

'Yes – and I had each matter looked into,' said Hall.

'So, Mr Hall, on the last voyage was it reported to you that there were a series of electrical faults?'

'No,' replied Hall, adding, 'No serious electrical faults were reported.'

With a flourish Rosen lifted some papers from the ledge.

'Let me turn to your own skipper's affidavit, Mr Hall, which stated that during the trip to the fishing grounds, a winch had been seen sparking on a number of occasions. Also, the electrical system in the officers' accommodation had also been faulty.

'On a number of occasions wiring had been on fire and burnt out, and trouble had been experienced with the fusing system. Other wiring had also burnt out, had it not?'

Rosen waved the affidavit from which he read.

'This had not been at reported to me at the time,' Hall replied. 'And if the situation was as serious as the affidavit makes out, it should have been reported by wireless.'

Rosen snapped back, 'If there is a breakdown of the electrical system do you not think that a very serious matter!'

'It was probably a spark that was not extremely serious.'

Rosen pressed on.

'If there was a serious scorching this could lead to a serious fire if the fuses were found not to be functioning, do you not agree, Mr Hall?'

'I would agree that would be so.' Hall added. 'These matters should be reported to me if there was nothing on board that could be done to correct them. I consider that adequate steps must have been taken. Electrical failure does occur on trawlers, probably due to damp or vibration.'

The skipper's lawyer HM Loncaster rose and said, 'Skipper Sawyer said that the *St Finbarr* had met with incredibly heavy weather on her last voyage. It had taken about hours to get up to the Pentland Firth. Mr Hall, Skipper Sawyer did all he could at this fire, did he not?'

Hall had to agree.

'And when the *St Finbarr* sailed, were you satisfied, Mr Hall, that she was in all respects fit for the sea?'

'Yes, I was. I agree.'

Judge Bucknill took the moment to bring Hall's ordeal to an end. 'Perhaps, gentlemen, this would be a good time to adjourn for lunch?'[6]

Albert "Taff" Evans and his pal and cabinmate Paddy Tognola were next to give evidence. Evans was first up and told how he woke choking in his intensely hot cabin.

'I could not see any smoke at first but I could hear crackling and a kind of roaring. In the alleyway I saw flames coming from the greasers' cabin. The whole door was on fire and the flames were leaping across the alley as if they were being pushed out.

'I got up on to the deck to get my breath back and then back down the starboard side where there was a lot of greyish-blue smoke. I saw Eric Petrini carrying another crewman. It was Jeff O'Dell.

'I got back up to the bridge and the skipper took my knife from me to smash the glass on the emergency bell.

'The bridge started to fill with smoke and the flooring began burning. Me and the second engineer then left the skipper on the bridge telephoning.'

Evans went on to tell how he watched two crewmen try to launch the lifeboat but they could not because it was live with electricity, and the skipper told them to leave it and launch the life rafts. Dr Rosen asked Evans if he had experienced any electrical faults previously on the trip.

'The only faults were things like bulbs having to be changed due to breakage or wearing out with vibrations. The *St Finbarr* was very bad for vibration.'[7]

Paddy Tognola told how he had awoke struggling for breath in the same cabin as his pal: 'I was not capable of rousing anybody because I could not breathe. I saw flames coming from the greasers' cabin, which was the next but one to mine.'

Tognola went on to tell how he too ended up on the deck and had managed to fetch some overalls from the drying room as a lot of the men were shivering in the freezing cold.

Had he noted any electrical faults before the fire, Dr Rosen asked?

'Water used to get into the accommodation sometimes, but never into the light fittings.' Tognola considered some more. 'Although I have seen lights go out on the bulkhead.'

'Did you ever receive any instruction on firefighting and the like and was there enough safety equipment, in your opinion?'

'I have had firefighting training on other trawlers but not the *Finbarr*. But there was a life jacket for every bunk.'[8]

Rosen's next witness was third engineer George Grinlaw.

'Had you heard there had been electrical trouble in the crew accommodation area, Mr Grinlaw?'

'Only on two occasions, sir.'

'And was there anyone qualified as an electrical engineer to deal with these problems?'

'No, sir, but when any electrical problems came up one of us would deal with them.'

Sawyer's lawyer cut in: 'Mr Grinlaw, whose duty was it to deal with such problems?

'The engineers' duty, sir.'

'And if there was a grave electrical difficulty?'

'Then the chief engineer would report it to the skipper.'

'But the skipper was not expected to know the technicalities of that sort of thing, surely?'

'No, sir,' replied Grinlaw. 'No such happening occurred on the trip and I didn't envisage any form of electrical danger.'

Was there any chance that any of the men were 'under the influence of alcohol'?

'There was no sign of anybody being in the slightest way under the influence of drink. The fire was totally unexpected. I am just as puzzled about it now as I was at the time.' Towards the end of his evidence the engineer told how the atrocious weather made the rescue by the *Orsino* incredibly difficult.

'It was impossible to lash the life raft to the *Orsino* because the sea was so heavy. When somebody fell into the sea that was his lot. If lifebelts had been thrown from the *Orsino* they would have done no good.'

Bosun Eric Samms, the Canadian veteran, echoed the engineer's evidence and said the raft that contained the men was connected to the *Orsino* only by the painter's line that helped pull it near.[9] At this point, Judge Bucknill intervened.

'Gentlemen, this may be the right juncture to stop today's proceedings and discuss the legal matters brought up earlier.'

The "legal matters" referred to the court being asked to witness experiments on wiring identical to that of the *St Finbarr*. The owners' lawyers and those of the ship's contractors wanted the whole thing held *in camera*, i.e. without press or the court officials being there. Bucknill disagreed. He felt it better that the whole court entourage attended the laboratory, although the Press would be excluded. The judge did promise the full results would be entered into evidence the next day. With that, Judge Bucknill and the Court of Inquiry adjourned to W Broady and Son Ltd, Hull.

The chartered bus from East Yorkshire Motor Services picked up the court entourage and drove the mile or so to

English Street, off Hessle Road, a stone's throw from the fish docks.

The street was a mix of terraced houses, factories and fish curing plants. The motor coach pulled up outside the street's biggest factory and the entourage, led by Judge Bucknill, disembarked from the charabanc like a party of very well-dressed tourists. W Broady and Son Ltd, Hull, was as much as part of the city as the fishing industry itself. Entrepreneurial coppersmith William Broady founded the company in 1902. They were in the safety valve and taps business – and business was good. By 1938, they had a worldwide reputation and provided valves for the Royal Navy and other fleets around the globe. The company also specialised in component testing.

The court party was led through the factory to a lab room where a table was laid out with a series of sections of cable. At the end of the table were a couple of light fittings, next to which were some more cables.

The samples had been taken from the Hamlings trawler *St Giles* – the newly built sister ship to the *St Finbarr*, which had an identical electrical system.

Glaswegian electrical contract foreman John MacLean from Ferguson Bros (Port Glasgow) set up the samples, through which it was intended to put increasing amounts of power. The experiment was to be quite simple. Each wire sample was increasingly overloaded and the results were to be observed and noted for the court. The first cable section had thirty amps put through it.

After almost half an hour the party became restless. Nothing appeared to happen. MacLean touched the cable and reported, 'It's warm, gentlemen, and getting warmer.'

An observer from Broady's and one from the court confirmed MacLean's information.

The input was then increased to seventy amps. This time the result a bit more visible. In just five minutes a small flame flickered from the test cable.

The lab technician increased the amperage to eighty and, within three minutes, gas spewed from the wiring and burst into flames a minute later. The gas presented itself as light smoke. It smelled vaguely like petrol.

Amperage was steadily increased. At 150 amps, gas belched from the blazing cable in just seven seconds. Various members of the party reached for handkerchiefs to cover their mouths as MacLean extinguished the fiery wiring. Further along the lab table were two lightbulb fixtures. The first housed a 100-watt light and the second a 200-watt one.

MacLean and the lab technician set to work. They firstly got new cables to catch fire before inducing an arcing of the light fitting. Both the high-wattage bulb and the lower caused the gas that came from the burning cables to explode instantly. Blue-green flames flashed momentarily from the setup, before the duo extinguished it.

'Gentlemen, I think we may have seen enough,' Judge Bucknill decided.

The following morning, the good judge was true to his word; in the opening minutes of that day's hearing the details of the previous evening's experiments were made public. It was uncomfortable for the trawler owners, especially Hamlings' superintendent engineer Charles Fleming, who had told the court earlier that the cause of the blaze was 'conjecture' and that he 'did not think it was due to an electrical fault'. Judge Bucknill invited Board of Trade lawyer Richard Stone to reveal the results. The lawyer told the court that the wiring used in the setup at Broady's was a replica of that on the *St Finbarr* and had been standard issue for sixty years and approved by Lloyd's of London.

Stone detailed how that wiring caught fire and emitted explosive gas at various stages of the experiment.

After Stone's submission, Board of Trade expert, marine engineer Alan Radcliffe, who had carried out similar experiments earlier in the year as part of evidence gathering, told the court, 'Possibilities of cigarette smoking and a fault in a lower bunk fitting had been considered and these had been ruled out because the fire had reached such an extent in a short time.

'The possibility of carelessness in the crew through alcohol had been considered, and because of the small amount of drink consumed this was not considered a relevant contributory factor.

'The fire probably originated behind the deckhead linings and not in the cabin itself. The most likely place for the original ignition was behind the linings and smoke could have spread widely through the cabins through a void space between the ship's side and the linings.

'I carried out tests on two sets of cabling and the effects of overloading. Gas came from both ends of both sets of cable, like a concentration of cigarette smoke. I tested it with a match and it burst into flames.'

The *St Finbarr*'s first mate, Walt Collier, one of the three ship's officers who stayed aboard the vessel at risk of his own life, was next to be questioned by Lionel Rosen.

'Mr Collier, what is your opinion on the blaze that claimed your vessel?'

'I really do not know what caused the fire. I have no comment to make at all.'

'During your sixteen months with the *St Finbarr* were there ever any fire drills undertaken?

'No, sir.'

'Yet, despite this, both Skipper Sawyer and yourself signed the log to indicate that fire drills did take place?'

'Yes.'

'The rules are quite clear, Mr Collier. How often should such drills take place?'

'Once a fortnight, sir.'

'Yet you and the skipper had not carried out such drills, not even once. Is that true?

'Yes.'

'And it was never logged as to why the fire drills never took place, was it Mr Collier?'

'No, sir.'

Once Rosen had embarrassed the first mate into admitting his and his boss's failure to carry out fire drills, he added, 'Did you spot any fire incidents yourself?'

'Yes, sir, there was a fire in the after gantry of the vessel, which was put out and the fault corrected.'

'Anything else?'

'Yes, on another occasion just hours before the fire I saw sparks from around the davit of the lifeboat.'

'I gather it was like a firework display?'

'No. That is not how I saw it,' said the mate, his temper visibly rising.

'And did you report it?'

'I intended to but I never got the chance.'

'No further questions.'[10]

Radio operator David Redshaw, the man Tommy Gray had replaced, took to the stand.

'In your evidence, Mr Redshaw, you have stated you saw many electrical faults on the *St Finbarr*. How did these manifest themselves?'

'They were mainly connected with electric motors, but occasionally with lighting.' The former radio operator, who had been with the vessel from her second trip to her thirteenth inclusive, told Rosen that he carried out various repairs himself.

'Was it your duty to do this?'

'No, sir, it was not my duty to do this, but you go to sea as a crew, and if you can do a job and it will help someone else, you do it.'

'What sort of repairs did you do?'

'Some of the faults on the early voyages were in the forward crew accommodation. Water got between the ceiling panelling and forward crew escape. On the last voyage that I was on I smelled smoke.'

'And you investigated it as any sensible person would have, being concerned about it?' Rosen said.

'Yes, sir. I traced it to the chief engineer's cabin. The main deck headlight, the internal light fittings and the wiring were all burned out.'

'You did not return to the *St Finbarr*, did you?'

'No, sir.'

The owners' lawyer Barry Sheen QC cut in: 'If there had not been a change in employment policy you would have gone back, would you not?' Redshaw agreed and said he had been "on loan" to Hamlings, and that if he had stayed longer with the *St Finbarr* it would have adversely affected his superannuation with the Rediffusion subsidiary, Redifon Ltd, which had hired him out.

'Otherwise, yes, I would have been on that trip, sir.'[11]

Chief engineer Hughie Williams came to the dock ramrod straight, took his oath, and sat facing the judge.

Dr Rosen wasted no time. 'Why, Mr Williams, were the fire hoses not used?'

He got a direct, almost abrupt answer: 'One has to study the safety of the ship. One must appreciate that the ship was in a force-eight gale beam-on, and the capacity of the pumps is approximately fifty tons an hour. Within an hour of pumping indiscriminately into the accommodation the water that was in the ship could have been disastrous.'

'It could hardly be more disastrous…'

'Yes, it could. Twenty-odd men might have been lost!'

Rosen adopted a more subdued tone. 'It may be a choice of two evils when a thing is on fire. These hydrants were there to swamp the fire with water. I am not blaming you because anyone in this position would have been in great difficulty. We want to understand why, being in a position where the fire hydrants were, you did not put them on the blaze?'

The phlegmatic engineer answered, 'It's not a seaman's drill to pump water indiscriminately. It is the wrong action.

I could not have stood there and directed it. The heat was intense.'

'You are saying it was too hot to stay there?'

'Yes.'

'No further questions.'

Sawyer's lawyer, Loncaster, took over. Was there any way the hydrant could have been used efficiently? Did Williams at any time think the ship's electrics were a danger.

Williams was adamant. 'There was no possibility of making efficient use of the hydrant. At no time did I feel the ship was in danger by electrical trouble, and I did not think there was a danger of fire either.

'In this case the place just filled with smoke before anyone saw any flames. It would have been difficult to subdue that fire with any of the equipment.'[12]

Later, outside the court building, deckhand Paddy Tognola did not see the woman who attacked him until she had hit him. The young fisherman was headed across the road to the Burlington Tavern (known locally as the Witnesses' Arms) for a pint after a long day in court reliving his horror in the Grand Banks. The young, head-scarfed housewife broke off from a small crowd and ran towards him. Her arms flailed. The slightly built woman screamed, 'Why are you still here and my man's not?! Why? Why?!' Her soft fists hit Paddy's chest as she bawled. He put his hands up to deflect her and seconds later a few people from the woman's group pulled her back from the shocked young trawlerman.

'Sorry, mate,' said one of the men who had dragged the woman away. 'She's not herself, you know.'

'Yeah, ok, course,' Paddy stammered as the woman was taken away.

One of the fisherman's mates came over to him.

'What's all that about?'

'No idea,' said Paddy. 'I've never seen her before in my life.'

He lit the roll-up cigarette in his shaking hand as he walked off.[13]

The following morning it was Skipper Sawyer's turn to tell his version of what had happened on the vessel he had commanded. He told of a bleak, harsh struggle for days on end against relentless gales and freezing temperatures.

'It took us thirteen to fourteen days to reach the Labrador coast, when in normal conditions it would have taken six,' said the skipper.

'We started fishing but the cold was severe. There was only one time when the temperature rose above zero.' The trawler captain told how they failed to trawl on Christmas Eve and how, in the early hours of the next day, the fishing had to be abandoned.

Sawyer said, 'There was a cross sea. We had a terrific north-westerly still running. It was a confused sea, more than the weight of the wind. We abandoned the fishing and the trawl was stored at about 4am.' The skipper was giving his evidence in reply to questions from the judge. He told Bucknill that by the point he stowed the trawl he was forced to use hand-steering because of an equipment breakdown that had made steering far more difficult than usual. Sawyer told the court that he arranged for the men to have a Christmas drink.

'It was a dram of whisky each and a couple of bottle of beer each. The whisky only amounted to a "sneck lifter", your honour. Later, Jimmy Hamilton, one of the men later lost, wished me a Merry Christmas – so I arranged for the crew to come to the bridge for another drink before they all turned in.'

Sawyer went on to tell Bucknill how the fire gripped the ship in minutes.

'When I was told of the smoke I went down from the bridge to have a look and found it to be intense. It was as though everything was closing in. Everything was full of smoke and there was no air at all.

'I didn't realise how serious it was. Everything was happening so quickly. I didn't even know there was a fire. I knew there was smoke. All you could see was a red glow.' Sawyer told how, after he was blown from the wheelhouse, he saw the men at the lifeboat who had shouted to him that it was live with electricity.

'I got hold of one of the boat gripes [the mechanism that releases the craft] and it threw me back.'

Sawyer added that the previous night he had seen sparks fly from the davit with a few flashes.

'I have seen that sort of thing many a time on other ships. I did not think it serious.'

Board of Trade lawyer Richard Stone asked, 'Yet you had held no fire drills. Do you accept that?'

'Yes,' replied the skipper. 'I know we should have done these things, but we didn't do it. We had boat drills instead.'

'No further questions.'

The judge nodded to Sawyer. 'It was a rather unlucky voyage altogether, was it not?'

'Yes, sir.'[14]

Sawyer turned and faced Rosen from the witness box as the lawyer cut to the chase. 'If fire drills had been held, the fire would probably have been stopped in time to save the ship and certainly there would have been more lives saved. Is that not the case?'

'Nothing else could have been done to save any more of the crew.' Sawyer's anger stoked his replies. 'I definitely do not agree with you that somehow if there had been practices that all the men would have got to their fire positions immediately and gone into operation. One could not let water run haphazardly on ship.'

Sawyer explained that there was a danger that too much water in the wrong place could have turned the ship over.

Rosen pressed on. 'Why not attack the fire?'

'Because it was not possible to get the fire hoses out of the boxes. The heat was too intense.'

'Don't you think that if there had been regular practices the men would have been in a much better position to attack the fire?'

'No, it was too quick.'

'I put it you that the order to abandon ship was premature.' Sawyer's brow furrowed. 'How do you mean?'

'There was no need for the men to have been ordered to the boats to leave the ship. I am saying you ordered that before it was necessary to do so. In fact, it turns out that it was premature.'

The skipper was in a battle of words and of truth. He fought back. 'These men were inadequately clothed. They could not have lasted any amount of time.'

'The *St Finbarr* stayed afloat for forty-eight hours after the fire, and men travelled to the trawler from the *Orsino* several times.' Such were the facts. Rosen followed through with his killer blow. 'Your order to abandon ship meant two men drowned unnecessarily.'

Sawyer could barely contain his anger.

'They were drowned, but I am not taking the blame for that. If the order had not been given those men would have died on the *St Finbarr*. The chief engineer would not have lasted another half hour at the very outside.'

Sawyer's own lawyer cut in. Would the skipper describe the conditions at the exact time of the order?

'It was in complete darkness in a force-eight gale. The ship was going across a heavy swell and rolling very heavily. I am satisfied I did everything I possibly could. There was nothing humanly possible that anyone else, myself or any member of the crew could have done to help matters in any way.'

Sawyer stared straight at Rosen: 'I stayed on the bridge until I was blown off it!

'I extend my deepest sympathy to those who lost members of their family but I did my best.'

Loncaster then turned his attention to Rosen: 'Skipper Sawyer has been vigorously attacked in this court today in a way which seemed unkind to say the least.'[15]

Rosen's aggressive cross-examination had backfired somewhat, but he carried on with a robust summing-up to the crowded court in the final hours of the ten-day-long public inquiry.

'Skipper Tom Sawyer agreed in evidence that he had not held fire drills and that by not holding the fire drills the skipper had tied his hands behind his back. Ten men died in the blazing ship and two more in the rescue operations. It is to Skipper Sawyer's credit that he had been frank about not having had the drills. But this is not a peccadillo but a serious matter and should be treated as such and not glossed over.

'When the ship caught fire, he was not able to deal with the situation. It is now pretty clear that the cause of the fire was an electrical fault, probably in one of the lamp holders. I am not suggesting criminal fault or moral blame but I submit there was negligence and a lack of responsibility.

'There had been warnings and they were not heeded. It was a sophisticated ship with unsophisticated personnel. The chief engineer says he was an amateur electrician. Some of the electrical fittings were not in good order to a dangerous extent. With such a mass of electrical equipment aboard there should have been someone competent to deal with matters when they went wrong.' Sawyer's lawyer, Loncaster, replied with a robust defence of his client.

'The fact that Skipper Sawyer was chosen to command this new vessel proves he is a man of great competency and a man to be relied on. His hands were not tied behind his back as if he were sitting down on the bridge and could not care less. From being perfectly normal one minute, this disaster finished up in five or six minutes with the bridge melting.

'I have to concede that my client never held the fire drills and my client's failure in that respect will probably be a lesson to other people that they must do the drills. But Skipper Sawyer's courage was what could be expected from a man of great character, who was firm and fair with his crew. Perhaps but for his courage more lives might have been lost.'[16]

The Wreck Commissioner, Judge Peter Bucknill QC, then asked to hear a brief summing-up from each of the lawyers for the owners and the contractors who had fitted the *St Finbarr*. Michael Feeny, for the electrical company Campbell and Isherwood of Liverpool, offered, 'No-one could be sure that it was an electrical fault which started the fire. I have no quarrel with anyone who might say that an electrical fault did start it. But it is a hypothesis.' Barry Sheen QC, for the owners, added, 'The *St Finbarr* was a well-constructed and well-maintained ship. We are dealing with a vessel that spent six to eight weeks at sea under the most gruelling conditions and to expect such a ship to return to port without some faults is inconceivable. Whatever electrical faults there were, were minimal and whatever lessons will be learned as a result of the inquiry would be put into operation in the future.'

'At this juncture I think we can say we have heard all the relevant evidence,' the judge summarized. 'It is my intention now to adjourn the hearing to a date to be fixed when the full findings will be revealed.'

It was dark when the court hearing ended and outside the weather was cold and sleety. Men, mostly in hats and caps, buttoned up their raincoats and tightened scarves, and women did similarly while they made sure their children were wrapped up properly against the cold. A throng of lawyers, trawlermen, maritime experts, witnesses and fishing families made their way out from Court Three into Alfred Gelder Street. The corridor they crossed to get to the exit was empty. All those who had business in other courts had left more than an hour earlier. A council commissionaire locked the ornate gates as the last people left the Guildhall.

For young widow Jill Harrison, the hearing had been the first time she had left her home since her husband Tony had perished aboard the *St Finbarr*, almost a year earlier. With her was a baby whom she had laid in the Silver Cross Queen of the Road, a child carriage that had the build of a small tank, the sort of pram favoured by Mary Poppins – which could be seen by the score being hurriedly pushed down Hessle Road on the payday "pram races".

Her toddler Jane was warmly wrapped up, her mittened hand held tightly in her mother's. When she had sorted the children, Jill pushed through the crowd that minutes earlier had left the hearing. There was still a considerable number milling around as she negotiated her way. A tall, dark figure was silhouetted against the street lamp. He moved towards Jill. She recognised him as he drew near. It was Eric Petrini, one of her husband's shipmates. Eric was a neighbour, but Jill had not seen him since the disaster as she had been confined to her home, mostly sedated by her GP, such was the shock of her grief. She was only able to force herself to the hearing because her father and mother had accompanied her in their car.

She was waiting for her parents when Eric approached.

'Hi Jill, love, all right?'

'Aye, I'm ok thanks, Eric.'

In the fading light and drizzling sleet Jill did not notice the burns and scars on the skin V of the young deckhand's open-necked shirt.

'Can I see the bain*?' Eric said. He had pulled back the pram blanket under which the infant lay as he asked, and continued, 'By, that's a bonny bain.'

His tone changed to a hush.

He looked directly at Jill: 'He knew, you know. He told me about the message, did your Tony, when we had a dram that Christmas. The telegram you signed "Jillian" to let him know you were expecting. He was right made up. He told me you were having a bain. He knew he were gonna be a dad. I just thought you should know that he knew. Sorry I haven't said earlier, but I didn't… you know…'

'Yeah… I know.' Jill struggled to compose herself as the news hit home, and the tears welled up. She did not know what to say. Her tummy fluttered as she thought about her beloved Tony knowing he was going to be a daddy again. She stuttered her reply.

'I named the bain after him.'

'Tony? A little lad, eh?'

'No, a girl. It's Toni… with an "I".

---

* 'Bain' is Hull vernacular for a child; it's a local pronunciation of 'bairn' as used by Scots and northern English folk.

AFTERWORDS

The Wreck Commissioner's inquiry into the *St Finbarr* disaster made its findings public on November 13, 1967. It concluded that a build-up of explosive gas was ignited, causing the fireball explosion that wiped out ten men instantly. However, the inquiry also said that the super-modern stern trawler was in 'seaworthy condition with all equipment in efficient working order'. And although the report said no-one was to blame for the disaster, it went on to make dozens of safety recommendations.

Judge Peter Bucknill QC said in a written report, 'In the Court's opinion the fire originated in the deckhead lining [of the greaser's cabin] in the air space formed by the deck beams and by the wood grounds supporting the deckhead lining. [...] It appears to the Court that an earth fault existed in the vicinity of the lifeboat davit.'

The report continued, 'Combustible gas, originating from the cabling in the air space, built up to a point where it formed an explosive mixture, which was ignited by a spark and blew the deckhead down. The flash of the explosion would cause surface burning on the wood grounds and on the deckhead lining, and the forced ventilation blowing on the ceiling of the cabins would fan this quickly into a violent blaze.'

It was recorded that earth faults in the davit, combined with others in the deckhead lighting, allowed heavier than usual currents to flow, causing the overheating that led to the explosion. The explosive gas that built up was identified as isobutylene.[1]

(What the inquiry did not detail, as it probably was not aware, is exactly how powerful isobutylene is. In its pure form, it is used in the production of modern aviation fuel. It also emits a petroleum-like odour, which in normal circumstances would have given a warning of a build-up. However, given that the build-up on the *St Finbarr* was near the ship's engines, there was no way that anyone would have noticed given the smell of fuel that usually permeated the air below decks.)[2]

Bucknill also cleared skipper Sawyer of any blame for any loss of life, saying he 'was right in sending a part of his crew away to the *Orsino* when he did. The Court would also like to record its appreciation of the fine work done from *Orsino* and also from the *Sir Fred Parkes*.'

The report went on to criticise the lack of fire drills and the fact that Sawyer failed to carry them out, but then added that the fire that struck the *St Finbarr* was so powerful that such drills would have made no difference.

However, it recommended that fire detectors be fitted on all new fishing vessels from that day forward, and that trawler owners were to organise regular firefighting training courses for all crews in future too.

Bucknill also said that fire hoses should be better stored in more fire-resistant containers, and that all hose fittings should be standardized and fuse boxes marked 'in a fool-proof manner'. There were a further two pages of detailed health and safety recommendations for better fire training and more regular maintenance of electrical equipment on board all fishing vessels.

In spite of Dr Lionel Rosen's revelations over lack of fire drills on the doomed ship, skipper Tom Sawyer came out of this inquiry with his reputation intact. Indeed, the report praised the courage of the commander and the two ship's officers, chief engineer Williams and first mate Collier, who stayed with the stricken vessel after getting twelve men off the trawler.

It was considered that the 'behaviour of the skipper had been exemplary'. (Skipper Sawyer continued to sail for Hamlings for the remainder of his long and distinguished career.)[3]

Jill Taylor Harrison Long, whose life story is a core element of this book, is now seventy years old and lives in comfortable, quiet retirement in suburban west Hull. She has five grandchildren and six great-grandchildren. She remarried to John Long, a trawlerman who became a successful skipper and, after the fishing industry declined, worked in the Middle East where he died of a heart attack in 2001. Mr Long took Jane and Toni as his own daughters and the couple had two more children, John junior, born in 1971, and Kerry, born in 1970.

John Long junior died of leukaemia in 1991, aged just twenty – the same age as Jill's first husband was when he met his death in 1966. Mrs Long remains a volunteer with the Royal National Mission to Deep Sea Fishermen, a role she has held for more than fifty years. The organisation was the one for which David MacMillan, the man who broke the news of lost fishermen to many (including Jill), worked. Mrs Long was also active with the St Andrew's Dock heritage group (STAND), which, in 2017, raised a memorial to the lost trawlermen of Hull on the riverside land of the shopping centre upon which the great dock once stood.[4]

Brian Williams, the superstitious deckhand who refused to sail on the *St Finbarr* because of the three delays before finally sailing, later had his morbid premonition fears come true when he met a catastrophic death on board the Hull trawler *St Britwin* in 1973. He was decapitated when a piece of heavy equipment swung loose. Furthermore, his belief that 'bad things came in threes' proved further to be a self-fulfilling prophecy when Brian's two brothers both died aboard the Hull trawler *Boston Lincoln* shortly after he perished on the *St Britwin*. Harry and Terry Williams, aged thirty-six and thirty-seven respectively, joined that ship together, breaking another trawlerman's taboo about brothers being on the same vessel. On January 30, 1974, while fishing White Sea grounds, Terry was caught by a snapped cable which knocked him unconscious and sent him down the stern ramp into the sea. His younger brother Harry leapt into the icy waters after him. Both died. Their bodies were washed up together in Russia and later brought home in the hold of a cable-laying vessel, the *Lindisfarne*.[5]

Eric Petrini, the *St Finbarr* deckhand who tried in vain to carry his friend Jeff 'Chuck' O'Dell to safety, was haunted for the remainder of his life by nightmares about the incident. Mr Petrini died of throat cancer little more than a year before this book was written.

In one of the most poignant and difficult interviews this author has conducted, a voiceless Mr Petrini "spoke" via his wife Susan using signs and writing – and the patience of a loving wife – to share his remarkable story. Referring to the incident at the posh tailoring shop in Newfoundland after the disaster, Mr Petrini told how upon his return there was a bill awaiting him from the owners for the clothing bought there. However, when a local reporter contacted Hamlings about the matter, it was dismissed as a "mistake" and the demands were instantly withdrawn and hugely bad publicity avoided by the company.[6]

Hughie Williams, the brave chief engineer who stayed aboard the *St Finbarr* with her skipper and mate until he had to be stretched off in a rescue boat, was also haunted by the 1966 disaster, even though he had survived a shipwreck previously. Mr Williams never fully got over not being able to help the young boy who called out to him from the blazing corridor near the engine room of the stricken ship.

Until the day he died, Hughie Williams often thought of the lad that took a wrong turn to his death in the thick smoke of the fire that claimed his ship.[7]

For the remainder of his career the *St Finbarr's* mate Walt Collier never stayed home at Christmas, despite pleas from his family. His son Gordon, who was an infant in 1966, recalled, 'He never spent a single Christmas at home after this incident, something I didn't understand at the time as other families whose dads went to sea made a point of missing a trip to ensure they would be home for the holidays.

'As a kid, I remember once asking Dad why he wouldn't stay home and he told me he had to go as it was his calling.

'After he left I asked Mam, "What's he talking about? Why won't he stay home at Christmas? Would it be so bad to spend it with us?"

'That was when she told me Dad had survived a fire on his ship and said he felt he didn't deserve to celebrate Christmas after that.'

Walt Collier was the last man home from Newfoundland as he had to have surgery on a burst ulcer. This almost took his life just hours after he had helped so many of his men to safety.

Gordon Collier added, 'I recently found out from an aunt that on returning to Hull after the *St Finbarr* disaster, my father was informed that his mother had unfortunately passed away on New Year's Eve. I do not think he ever recovered fully.

'Dad left the family home unexpectedly when I was 15 years old and about to leave school in June 1980.

'He came home sat me down and said I was a man now and able to make my own way in the world. This came as a complete shock to Mam as they had no marital problems that she knew of. I saw him only once after that, a few weeks later, just after my sixteenth birthday.

'He went down to Lowestoft to work on oil rig support vessels. I was told by my Auntie Lucy that a few years later he was sleeping on the beach as he had no accommodation and I was greatly upset by this.

'My mother took this very badly at the time and it was difficult for me too as I was the only one of his three children still at home so had to deal with Mam's loss. He wouldn't engage in conversation and only ever rang Mam to tell her if he wasn't working.

'He never saw any of his six grandchildren. I was informed of my dad's death some eight years later but it was three days after his funeral. Even his sister Lucy didn't know until this time that Dad had passed.

'He had had a heart attack two years previously at the age of sixty-one. Doctors had stopped him sailing by then and sadly he died a stranger to me at the age of sixty-three.

'This was a sad time for our family and my middle sister spent a couple of years looking for him, even taking all her holidays to search around Lowestoft, but to no avail.

'We do not know the circumstances of what went on after he left but his sister Lucy still believes he never recovered from the loss of *St Finbarr* and that of his mother shortly afterwards.'

Whether it was survivor's guilt or remorse over the signing of false fire drill reports that plagued Walt Collier, we will never know. Only Mr Collier knew that inner truth.

What we do know is that the man's courage helped save many of his shipmates' lives.

Paddy Tognola is now in his mid-seventies and lives in retirement by the sea in the East Yorkshire resort of Withernsea. To this day he is angry with the owners of the ship for a promise he says they had broken. Despite the reassurances given by the firm when the men were on their way home to Hull from Newfoundland that they would be paid in full, Mr Tognola arrived home to nothing. 'We were promised full pay. I don't know about the others, but I got nothing. Oddly, they gave me another job with Skipper Sawyer on his next command, the *St Giles*. I could not protest, really. I had to make a living, didn't I?'

George William Lee, the radio operator whose photographs of the *St Finbarr* disaster remained in an album kept by his family until the publication of this book, died in a later Christmas Day fishing disaster. Mr Lee was wireless operator on Hull trawler H396 *Ian Fleming*. He died on December 25, 1973, off the coast of Norway when the ship on which he served struck rocks and sank. Mr Lee was among three men to have died of exposure in the freezing waters when the raft he was in with the skipper and mate had capsized due to being improperly inflated. Three rafts were launched in total. The skipper survived. It was suspected that there had been a misuse of alcohol and that the skipper may have been drunk and had allowed the men to drink too much. The Court of Inquiry at the time sought to cancel his certificate of command, but relented because there was no concrete evidence as to what was drunk by whom. The skipper, David Atkinson, was suspended for three years.[8]

The request from Harry "Curly" Smith's widow Ivy to have him buried at sea in 1966 splits the family to this day.

Jonathan Watson Hall, the trawler company executive who flew to Newfoundland to help his stricken men, now lives in quiet retirement on his farm in East Yorkshire. A little more than a year after the *St Finbarr* explosion, another

Hamlings ship, the *St Romanus*, met a mysterious end and was the first of three ships to sink in the 1968 Hull Triple Trawler Disaster.

It is estimated that in a century more than 6,000 trawlermen sailed from Hull never to return. Deep-sea fishing was the most dangerous occupation on Earth. Behind the thousands of lost lives are tens of thousands more that were, and are to this day, blighted. On Christmas Day, 1966 there was another tragedy involving a Hull trawler. George Henry Smith, twenty-nine, a sparehand on the Hamlings ship *St Alcuin*, was lost overboard returning from the White Sea. It was George's fifth trip on that trawler. George's father, also called George Henry was lost at sea years earlier. The tragic trawlerman was the third generation to go to sea. The *St Alcuin's* skipper, Jack Nelson, searched for hours in vain to try to find the lost fisherman. *St Finbarr* disaster widow Jill Long recalled reading in the local paper of that tragedy and said it saddened her deeply even though she never knew the deckhand who disappeared, but she was friends with his wife, Pat.

She said, 'I remember thinking that this man would somehow be overlooked as it were, because of the tragedy of the *St Finbarr*. After all, the death of one man is as big a tragedy to his family as the death of many elsewhere. It sounds silly, I know, but I remember feeling at the time that I hoped people would remember this poor man as much as they did our men.'

The *St Alcuin* had been Skipper Sawyer's first command. It was the ship after which he named his house.

Fewer than ten weeks after the inquiry into the *St Finbarr* disaster made its findings public, the biggest peacetime fishing catastrophe of the twentieth century struck the Hessle Road community. In what became known as the Dark Winter of 1968, three ships, the *St Romanus*, the *Kingston Peridot* and the *Ross Cleveland* sank within as many weeks with the loss of fifty-eight men. One man survived – Harry Eddom, the mate of the *Ross Cleveland*, who struggled for thirty-six hours in the frozen wastes of Iceland before being found by a shepherd boy. His return to Hull brought the world's media attention to the city and the industry. This, coupled with an uprising of Hull fishwives led by Lillian Bilocca, aka Big Lil, took Vietnam off the front pages. Together with Mary Denness, Yvonne Blenkinsop and Christine Smallbone, Mrs Bilocca was responsible for a wildcat campaign that resulted in massive safety changes for the trawling industry: an immediate ban on fishing in atrocious weather in the Arctic, better weather forecasting, improved training (especially for young crewmen) and, for the first time in the history of fishing, the British fleet had a 'mother ship' appointed as a hospital and weather vessel combined. The full story of the Triple Trawler Disaster is told in *The Headscarf Revolutionaries* (Barbican Press, 2015). That disaster overshadowed the story of the 'forgotten men of *St Finbarr*' – a situation which hopefully this book has helped to rectify.

The 'mother ship' that appointed to the fishing fleet for the first time after the 1968 uprising was the *Orsino*, under the command of skipper Eddie Wooldridge.

WHAT THEY SAID ABOUT
THE HEADSCARF REVOLUTIONARIES:

'Best book written from Hull. Ever.'

> **– Russ Litten**, Hull-based novelist, poet,
> publisher and musician. Author: *Swear Down,*
> *Scream if You Want to Go Faster* and *Kingdom.*

'I love, love, love, this book! The story of Big Lil and the Headscarf Revolutionaries inspires me.'

> **– Jess Phillips MP**, author, *Everywoman – One*
> *Woman's Truth About Speaking the Truth.*

'Hull's "headscarf revolutionaries" could inspire the next big British drama.'

> **– Dean Kirby,** *The Independent.*

'As the cliché goes, I just could not put *The Headscarf Rev-olutionaries* down. And it is all credit to Glasgow journalist Brian W Lavery for making this somewhat niche subject so riveting.'

> **– Ines Watson,** *Scottish Sunday Express*

'Brian's story made me feel as if I was back in the fight in 1968. It was almost like he had been with us. By far and away the best thing ever written about us.'

> **– Mary Denness** (1937-2017) – trawler safety
> campaigner, one of the Headscarf Revolutionaries.

'This is a story of the men whose exploits built a city's wealth and helped feed a nation. Lavery's tale of how the Triple Trawler Tragedy unleashed the fury of the formidable women of Hessle Road is inspirational.'

– **Alan Johnson,** former MP for West Hull and Hessle.
Author, *This Boy*, *Please Mister Postman* and
The Long and Winding Road.

'Mark my words, this could be become the next *Made in Dagenham*. Lily Bilocca was remarkable.'

– **Lord John Prescott,** former Labour
Deputy Prime Minister and MP for East Hull.

'With a novelist's eye for colour and detail, he brings alive the fishing industry of the 1960s... The scenes at sea are as vivid as anything in Hemingway or Melville, and winter conditions in Icelandic waters make life at Alistair Maclean's *Ice Station Zebra* seem tame. *The Headscarf Revolutionaries* is an enthralling read [...] and an important addition to working-class history.'

– **DD Johnston,** author, *Peace, Love and Petrol Bombs*,
The Deconstruction of Professor Thurb,
The Secret Baby Room and *Disnaeland.* – via *libcom.org*

'The story of the Hessle Roaders who took their fight all the way to the corridors of power in Parliament deserves to be known throughout the UK. For too long, the achievement of the women, like the city in which they lived, has been overlooked. Dr Lavery should be congratulated for telling their story in such a gripping way and his achievement in securing the interests of the production company is to be celebrated.'

– *Hull Daily Mail*

'This is compelling and detailed account of ordinary women changing history. […] This is a powerful book.'

– **Sarah Ensor**, *Socialist Review* magazine.

'Lavery goes into detail about the personal circumstances of the key players in this story. […] It is genuinely moving.'

– **Steve Regan**, *Northern Soul*, Manchester arts website

ACKNOWLEDGEMENTS

I owe an immeasurable debt to Jill Long, the then young wife of deckhand Tony Harrison who was left widowed, with a baby, also pregnant and not yet nineteen. Without her, this story would be much less than it is. I want to thank her for allowing me to dramatise some of the most tragic parts of her life. Her kindness and patience over the years have proved to be invaluable. Mrs Long's sharing of the lifestyles of the time, her detailed assistance and her advice proved indispensable. We have known each other for more than five years and it was while she helped me with a previous book that this story came to my attention and I could not let it go.

Patrick 'Paddy' Tognola, survivor of the *St Finbarr* tragedy, also kindly gave of his time and expertise to allow me to put together some of the most detailed and dramatic parts of this story. He recounted the most devastating time of his life at sea and did so with great generosity. His technical advice was also great value.

I am also grateful to the late Eric Petrini, the brave deckhand who tried in vain to rescue his friend from the blazing ship. In the final days of his life he had lost his voice and with the help of his wife Susan managed to tell me his story in one of the most harrowing interviews I have conducted. Eric's cousins, former trawlerman Graham Petrini and Susan Ward, added to the immense amount of information gathered for this story.

Gordon Collier, whose father Walt was mate on the *St Finbarr,* assisted me greatly too.

Special thanks go to Dave Linkie, Katharine Weir and Rachel Graham of the industry newspaper *Fishing News* for providing archive cuttings and giving generously of their time.

My thanks go to retired Hull trawler skippers Ray Hawker, Ken Knox and Peter Craven for sharing their expertise. But I am especially thankful to Skipper Hawker, who spent hours over many months, advising me in details about not only the technical aspects of his profession, but also recounted his eyewitness accounts of the *St Finbarr* disaster from his vantage point as a young deckhand aboard the *Ross Illustrious.* Retired trawlerman Ray Coles, who along with Skipper Hawker, is a leading light in the Hull Bullnose Heritage Group, was also a limitless fount of knowledge about the industry and many of the characters from it, now gone.

Each time I called either of the "two Rays" they were always helpful and never stinted in the sharing of their stories, advice, anecdotes and vast maritime expertise.

Similarly, retired ship's engineer Dusty Miller, a witness to the disaster, gave not only details of his experience on that day, but also technical advice on the powering of a stern trawler.

My dear friend Max Gold, who passed away in May this year, spent a lifetime as a doyen of Hull's legal profession. He was the key legal adviser to the families of the lost trawler *Gaul*. He spent many years supporting the bereaved in the hunt for the truth about this lost ship. His help in enabling me to draw the character of another great Hull lawyer, the late Dr Lionel Rosen, was incomparable.

I also owe thanks to Jonathan Watson Hall, the former trawler owner, who kindly gave of his time and answered difficult questions with good grace.

James Mitchell and Rob Stebbing, former and present picture editors respectively of my old paper the *Hull Daily Mail*, could not have been more helpful both in the swift and courteous answering of queries and the provision of photos for this book.

The distinguished Hull maritime historian Dr Robb Robinson, as always, was on hand to help. A brilliant mind and a fine chap, Dr Robinson is like a wise, human historical search engine to whom I owe a great debt. My thanks go also to Professor Hugh Murphy, visiting reader in maritime history at the National Maritime Museum, Greenwich, and the Centre for Business History in Scotland at the University of Glasgow; as well as Professor Lewis R "Skip" Fischer, of the Department of History at the Memorial University of Newfoundland, for pointing me in the right direction. Special thanks indeed go to the man they pointed me to – Kory Penney, archivist for the Maritime History Archive at the Memorial University of Newfoundland, whose kind assistance, provision of numerous news cuttings and archive material and advice added greatly to the Canadian side of this story.

Similarly, the Hull History Centre proved indispensable as always – a true jewel in our culture city. I would like to thank further the Hull Bullnose Heritage Group, for access and use of material from its website and Ray Coles (again!) for accessing records and information on my behalf.

Special thanks must go to Gavin Gray, son of Tommy Gray, the radio operator who died in the *St Finbarr* rescue operation, and Ron Smith, son of Harry "Curly" Smith, the greaser who died in the same rescue attempt.

Both men provided time, help, information and photographs for this book.

Also, Alan Burgin, stepson of Jack Smith, the fish room chargehand who perished in the fire, was one of the first to help me with the research for this story.

Former Hull MPs John Prescott and Alan Johnson were most helpful too – especially John, who allowed me to be the first person to access his papers lodged with the University of Hull. At the time, these papers were not even catalogued fully. John and Alan were of help both for this book and my previous one. I also appreciate John's time visiting me and going through old copies of the radical Hull union newspaper *Humberside Voice*.

Vanessa Olsen, daughter of the late George William Lee, the radio operator whose photographs from the disaster helped to illustrate this book, kindly gave permission for those images to be reproduced.

Thank you to the daughters of the *St Finbarr* chief engineer – Linda Drury, Jeanette Upfold and Paula Marshall – for collectively sharing the story of their father's life. Musicians – Mick McGarry, Keith Gay, Brian Nelson,

"Wakefield Kev", Les Ward, and the regulars at the Wednesday folk sessions at the Ye Olde Black Boy pub in Hull's Old Town (where I seek refuge from work) – have my gratitude for equal measures of comradeship and Talisker – and for putting up with my shocking lack of musicality. Brian Nelson allowed me to reproduce his lyrics from *Fishing with Ocean Liners* (inspired by a story from Les Ward) from the McGarry-Nelson album *Flowers on the Water*.

Keith Gay, another fine musician and writer of the Hull trawlerman's anthem *Settling Day*, allowed reproduction of his lyrics and contributed to several interviews. He is the nephew of Skipper Philip Gay, of the ill-fated *Ross Cleveland*.

The late Hull skipper Jimmy Williams, who previously gave so much help in my research, provided me with knowledge and advice that will be with me all my days. If I have forgotten anyone, then please forgive me.

My wife Kathryn and my daughters Catriona and Rose have my perpetual love and thanks, especially my poor Kathryn, who has the unenviable tasks of being an unpaid editor and proof-reader.

The author also wishes to thank the Denness family for their kind permission to reproduce the poem "Maggie" written by the late Mary Denness, trawler safety campaigner and activist.

And finally, my publisher, editor and friend, Martin Goodman of Barbican Press, a man whose kindness, patience and skill merits the world of thanks I owe him.

Maggie

(The Past)

The mission man came to our house today
I didn't know what to do, I didn't know what to say.
The mission man knelt and started praying
But I couldn't take in a word he was saying.
I sent the bairn to get his mam
Whilst I saw to the little one in his pram.
The lassies in the terrace began to gather
I invited them in, and we all wept together.
But, I knew days ago now I'd never see Billy any more
I'd walked Hessle Road, I'd seen the faces
The cold, still air, the questioning grimaces
I went back home and closed my door and whispered
Ta-rah Billy forever more.

(The Present)

Where have you gone to Billy lad?
You're somewhere out there with your poor old dad
Both of you lost years ago now, they never knew why, they
    never knew how.
The bairns have grown up big and strong
They ask about you and where they belong.
Your mam's still with us, she still feels the pain
Looks out to seaward again and again.
We're all growing older Billy lad, and if there is just one
    thing I wish I had
It's another resting place for you instead of the sea.
Where I could put flowers and in my reverie
Be alone with you for a while Billy lad
To talk about the tomorrows we never had.

Hold fast the hatch of memory's montage
The future is waving the past 'bon voyage'.

– **Mary Denness**, *1937-2017,*
trawler safety campaigner, social activist,
Headscarf Revolutionary – and poet. RIP. 'Lux perpetua'

ENDNOTES

PROLOGUE

1 Tunstall, Jeremy. *The Fishermen – the sociology of an extreme profession* (Macgibbon and Kee, London, 1962), pp. 17-19.

2 Tunstall, *The Fishermen*, p. 21

3   Robinson, Robb. *Trawling – the rise and fall of the British Trawl Fishery* (University of Exeter Press, 1996), pp. 32-33.

4 Thompson, *A Tribute to Hull's Fishing Industry* (Hutton Press, 1996), pp. 10-11.

5 Thompson, *A Tribute*. pp. 12-13. (Their fears turned out to be even worse than feared and in 1975, the Icelandic unilaterally declared a 200-mile limit and a year later the British Government recognised the Icelandic demands, dealing a gigantic blow to the British trawl fishery and wiped out the giant Hull fleet.)

CHAPTER ONE

1 The author is grateful to Jill Long, widow of Tony Harrison, the deckhand who perished on the *St Finbarr*. Over the past few years, Mrs Long has been of invaluable assistance with the author's work. The writer is particularly grateful for her understanding and permission to dramatise parts of her life and those of her family.

CHAPTER TWO

1   'Don skipper' is a colloquial term for a trawler commander of very high repute.

2   Fishermen's Friend website and Fleetwood source.

3   This anecdote was recounted by Jonathan Watson Hall in his recorded interview with the author.

4   From 'When new "Saint" is sailing in…' *Hull Daily Mail*, September 25, 1966. (Article by Robert S Wellings)

5   Credland, Arthur, *Fishing the Humber* (The History Press, 2014), p. 113.

CHAPTER THREE

1   A 'doxy' was the name given to what was then called a 'good time girl' – not quite a hooker, as often money did not change hands, although drinks and presents certainly did, usually from the hands and wallets of many a 'cherry boy' fisher lad.

2   A reference to Ken Loach's first film, made for the BBC, which aired that night. *Cathy Come Home* shocked the British public with its stark revelations of homelessness in 1960s Britain.

3   Again, the author is grateful to Jill Long, widow of Tony Harrison, for the details provided and for the time she has spent ensuring the details are accurate.

CHAPTER FOUR

1   In what became known as the Russian Outrage of 1904, part of the Hull trawler fleet was sunk in atrocious weather by the Russian Navy, which mistook the fishing vessels for the Japanese Navy. There is a statue on the corner of Hessle Road and Boulevard to the men of the Gamecock Fleet involved in the incident, which almost brought the two countries to war.

2   Brian Williams' story was told to the author by Jill Long, as part of a series of interviews. The writer is also grateful for details from the hulltrawler.net website on this story too.

3   Details of ship's supplies from Hamlings Papers, archived at the Hull History Centre.

4   *Hull Daily Mail*, page one, 'Faults on trip after trip' – September 20, 1967.

5   Board of Trade wreck report for *St Amandus*, 1948 (HMSO) and *Trawler Disasters 1946-1975*, by John Nicklin and Patricia O'Driscoll (Amberley Publishing, 2010), p18.

6   The author is grateful to the daughters of chief engineer Hughie Williams for taking the time to share the story of their lives with their heroic father.

7   Wilson, Keppel and Betty were a British vaudeville act. Ironically one of the trio Joe Keppel ended his days in the St Finbarr Care Home in his native Cork. The author is grateful to Harry Smith's son, Ron Smith, for granting interviews and providing extra information as well as photographs.

8   From an interview with Keith Gay, nephew of the *Ross Cleveland* skipper Philip Gay. Keith is also the songwriter of the fishermen's anthem *Settling Day*. The author is grateful for his assistance.

CHAPTER FIVE

1   JT Edson (John Thomas Edson, 1928-2014) was an immensely popular English author of escapist western literature.

2   Interviews with Alan Burgin (stepson of Jack Smith). The author is grateful to Mr Burgin for sharing his experiences and allowing them to be reproduced in this book.

3   'Eighteen in three families lose a father' – *Hull Daily Mail*, December 28, 1966.

4   The author is grateful to Ray Coles of the Hull Bullnose Heritage Group for retrieving the sailing records of Jack Smith of the *St Finbarr* – and again to Mr Smith's stepson Alan Burgin for additional materials.

5   'St Finbarr Inquiry told: Faults on "trip after trip"' *Hull Daily Mail*, September 20, 1967.

6   Retrieved online from newworldencylopedia.org.

7 Thanks to retired Hull trawler skipper Ray Hawker, retired fisherman Ray Coles and the late Hull skipper Jimmy Williams for details of trawler operations and fishing grounds. Without men like these my work would be lacking much.

8 'St Finbarr engineer smelled smoke: Probe told of charred cable' – *Hull Daily Mail*, September 21, 1967.

9 Report of Court (No. S437) s.t. St Celestin, O.N. 1851129 s.t Arctic Viking, O.N. 165649, August 3, 1956. Judge: Waldo Porges.

10 'Mate tells inquiry: Fire drills "never held on St Finbarr"' – *Hull Daily Mail*, September, 19, 1967. And interviews with family and friends. Ibid. Report of Court No. S478, m.f.v. St Finbarr (ON 305772), November 13, 1967.

11 From interviews with Jill Long, widow of deckhand Tony Harrison.

CHAPTER SIX

1 *The Headscarf Revolutionaries* by Brian W. Lavery. (Barbican Press, 2015). p18.

2 Report of Court of inquiry (S478) m.f.v. St Finbarr 1967, page three.

3 Testimony of Paddy Tognola reported in the *Hull Daily Mail*: 'Quiet drinks, sleep…then – the fire…' – September 21, 1967. Also, pp. 1-2, report of Court. And interviews with Mr Tognola by the author.

CHAPTER SEVEN

1 Report of Court of Inquiry (S478) m.f.v. St Finbarr 1967, pp. 2-4.

2 This incident haunted Williams for the remainder of his life. The author is grateful for his family sharing the story, which had affected Mr Williams so badly.

3 'St Finbarr inquiry told: men could not launch boat' – *Hull Daily Mail*, September 21, 1967. Plus, interviews with the family of chief engineer Hughie Williams. And interviews with Paddy Tognola, former St Finbarr deckhand.

4 'Finbarr survivors' grim fight for life' (inquiry report) *Hull Daily Mail*, September 29, 1967.

5   *Hull Daily Mail*, December 29, 1966, front page. '10 trawlermen died instantly in rush of flame; Skipper's tragic story – St Finbarr survivors' grim fight for life.'

6   *St John's Daily News*, December 30, 1966. 'Orsino radio operator tells of dramatic sea rescue', as told to Dave Butler, News Staff Writer. Also grateful to Sue Ward (cousin to the late Eric Petrini) for added details.

7   Mayo clinic website.

CHAPTER EIGHT

1   The writer is immensely grateful to retired Hull skipper Ray Hawker, then a young deckhand on the *Ross Illustrious* that fateful Christmas Day, for his constant assistance and guidance in the telling of this story.

2   Thanks again to Ray Hawker for guidance and advice in the practicalities of employing rescue techniques, for eyewitness reports from the disaster and for seemingly endless patience with nuisance enquiries from the author!

CHAPTER NINE

1   This chapter has been synthesised from the official court of inquiry report (Report of Court No. S478, m.f.v. St Finbarr (pp 1-6) – as well as the following articles from the *St John's Daily News*: 'Captain describes Finbarr tragedy,' – page 1, December 28, 1966; 'Orsino radio operator tells of dramatic sea rescue' – December 30, 1966; 'Skipper's tragic story – St Finbarr survivors' grim fight for life' – *Hull Daily Mail*, first edition, December 28, 1966. Also, information was used from interviews with Paddy Tognola, former deckhand on the *St Finbarr*, and Ray Hawker, retired skipper, then a sparehand on the Hull trawler *Ross Illustrious*, who saw the tragedy unfold.

CHAPTER TEN

1 From interviews with Jill Long, widow of Tony Harrison, deckhand, the *St Finbarr*.

2 From interviews with Alan Burgin, stepson of Jack Smith, charge-hand, the *St Finbarr*.

3 The Hotham Papers, Hull History Centre (U DDHO/1).

4 Details from '24 hours of agony for crew's families' – *Hull Daily Mail*, December 28, 1966.

5 From interview: Jill Long.

CHAPTER ELEVEN

1 Details from '24 hours of agony for crew's families' – *Hull Daily Mail*, December 28, 1966.

2 'Orsino radio operator tells of dramatic sea rescue', by WE Dunn as told to Dave Butler – *St John's Daily News*, December 30, 1966.

3 Ibid – *St John's Daily News*, December 30, 1966.

4 From the Hamling Papers archived at the Hull History Centre.

5 Barbara Robinson, *Hull Daily Mail, A Part of the Community* (Hull Daily Mail Publications, 2010). A section of this booklet entitled the 'Mister from the Mail' is dedicated to the more ethical and sympathetic approach, especially with the fishing community, compared to the practices of the national press and other media organisations. Also, as a young man, the author worked for the *Hull Daily Mail* as the reporters of this era were late in their careers.

6 From interviews with Jill Long, formerly Jill Harrison, widow of Tony Harrison, deckhand on the *St Finbarr*. Once more the author expresses his thanks for Mrs Long taking the time to assist and to allow her life to be dramatised.

CHAPTER TWELVE

1 Telegram from the Hamling Papers stored at the Hull History Centre. Details of the sinking from eyewitness reports by skipper Sawyer and *Orsino* radio operator Bill Dunn to the *St John's Daily*

News reporters Jack Fitzgerald and Dave Butler. The author is also grateful to Dusty Miller, retired trawler engineer for taking time to tell his story and for his assistance in the answering of technical questions.

2   From 'Captain Describes Finbarr Tragedy – Survivors of Sea Disaster Arrive Aboard Sister Ship (Dept. of Transport Inquiry Scheduled Today)' by Jack Fitzgerald. (*The Daily News*, St John's Newfoundland, Thursday, December 28, 1966.)

3   Waistell's was a renowned Hessle Road tailor's shop well used by the fishermen as was the 'fifty-bob tailor' Manny Marx, who traded as Southwell's of Hull.

4   The author is grateful again to Paddy Tognola, deckhand from the *St Finbarr*, for his best efforts to recollect this part of the story. Without Mr Tognola's help the telling of this story would have been much diminished.

5   From 'Orsino radio operator tells of dramatic sea rescue,' by WE Dunn, as told to Dave Butler, News Staff Writer – *The Daily News*, St John's, December 30, 1966.

6   From a serialisation in *The Telegram* (St John's), September 19, 2016, of *Amazing and Strange, Jack Fitzgerald's Treasury of Newfoundland Stories, Vol II* (accessed online March 2017).

7   'We were a family, not a crew,' – page five, *Hull Daily Mail*, December 31, 1966.

8   The author is grateful to the daughters of chief engineer Hughie Williams for sharing their memories of their father's life and times.

CHAPTER THIRTEEN

1   From the records of Historic England (List entry Number: 1279708) accessed online April 17, 2017.

2   Page one, Report of Court, No. S478, m.f.v. St Finbarr (ON 305772).

3   The author wishes to thank his friend, the distinguished Hull lawyer Max Gold, a leading member of the city's Jewish community, for his time and knowledge of the life and times of Dr Lionel Rosen, also for his advice on maritime law and practice.

4 'Deckhands' lucky escape – blaze was beyond control, Hull inquiry told' – *Hull Daily Mail*, September 19, 1967; 'Crew awoke to find a blazing inferno – *Fishing News*, September 29, 1967.

5 'Electrical fault theory in St Finbarr probe – QC tells of "blow lamp effect"' – page four, *Hull Daily Mail*, September 20, 1967.

6 'St Finbarr inquiry told – faults on "trip after trip"' – *Hull Daily Mail*, page one, September 20, 1967.

7 'St Finbarr inquiry told – men could not launch lifeboat' – *Hull Daily Mail*, page one, September 21, 1967

8 'St Finbarr inquiry told of shivering men, black smoke' – *Hull Daily Mail*, September 22, 1967; 'St Finbarr inquiry', *Fishing News*, pp. 4-5, October 6 edition, 1967.

9 'Survivors tell tragic story of St Finbarr – quiet drinks, sleep… then – the fire…' – page five, *Hull Daily Mail*, September 22, 1967. Also in part from *Fishing News*, October 6, 1967.

10 'Fire drills "never held on St Finbarr"' – page one, *Hull Daily Mail*, September 23, 1967.

11 'Carried out repairs at sea – radio operator tells of faults' – page five, *Hull Daily Mail*, September 23, 1967.

12 'Finbarr toll could have been higher' – page three, *Hull Daily Mail*, September 28, 1967.

13 Based on one of a series of interviews with Paddy Tognola, former deckhand on the *St Finbarr*, for which the author is immensely grateful.

14 'Skipper tells of St Finbarr's last hours' – page six, *Hull Daily Mail*, September 28, 1967.

15 'St Finbarr inquiry allegations – Skipper denies "abandon" order was premature' – page one, *Hull Daily Mail*, September 28, 1967.

16 'St Finbarr – "Skipper tied his hands" – Dr Rosen' – page one, *Hull Daily Mail*, September 29, 1967. All the reports cited from the *Hull Daily Mail* were also complemented by those from the trade newspaper *Fishing News*, which are referred to throughout. The author wishes to thank David Linkie and Katherine Weir from that newspaper's current online incarnation for providing so many archives. That provision proved invaluable.

AFTERWORDS

1 From Report of Court No. S478 – m.f.v. St Finbarr (ON 305772) – November 13, 1967.

2 The author is grateful to Prof. Mark Lorch from the University of Hull's chemistry department for initial guidance and would like also to record the c-f-c.com website's information on isobutylene gas.

3 From Report of Court No. S478 – m.f.v. St Finbarr (ON 305772) – November 13, 1967, also; *Fishing News*, November 1967.

4 From interviews with Jill Long.

5 From interviews with Jill Long; also, hulltrawlernet.com (accessed May 2, 2017).

6 Interviews with Eric Petrini, former deckhand of the *St Finbarr* (now deceased), and his widow Susan Petrini, and Graham Petrini, cousin to Eric.

7 From interviews from the family of the late Hughie Williams, chief engineer of the *St Finbarr*.

8 *Trawler Disasters*, p171-172.

Printed in the USA
CPSIA information can be obtained
at www.ICGtesting.com
JSHW012230150923
48612JS00001B/1

9 781909 954861